Surviving Separation and Divorce

Surviving Separation and Divorce

Dealing with divorce day-to-day

Ruth Clements

LION

Published by
Lion Hudson Limited
Wilkinson House, Jordan Hill Business Park
Banbury Road, Oxford OX2 8DR, England
www.lionhudson.com

ISBN 978 0 7459 8074 4
e-ISBN 978 0 7459 8075 1

First edition 2019

A catalogue record for this book is available from the British Library

Printed and bound in the UK, July 2019, LH26

To the Bishops,
my second family – thank you for taking me in,
building me back up, and always welcoming me home.
And to Ellie – because finding I wasn't the
only one in this situation gave me hope.

Acknowledgments

Over the years the support I have received through marriage, divorce, and life after that has been immeasurably generous and invaluable. Thank you to everyone who has played a part in that. Here is a tiny summary of my thanks. No words will ever be sufficient to explain what it has meant, and continues to mean, to me.

With regard to the book itself, a huge thank you to Erik Castenskiold for his generous introduction, and to Suzanne Wilson-Higgins, Jon Oliver, and all at Lion Hudson for their belief in me and the impact this book could have. To the wonderful contributors – Row, Ellie, May, Carol, and Decobe – thank you not only for your contributions but also for your collective wisdom, encouragement, and support over the years. Thank you, Liza Hoeksma, for your advice several years ago, and for taking the time to meet a stranger. Thank you to Siobhan Hooper for being my creative sounding board, and to Ellie Cross, Tim Bechervaise, Jennie Pollock, Dad, Phil, and anyone else I've forgotten for the regular reading and literary advice.

To my wonderful family: Mum, Dad, "the boys" (Ben, Tom, and Joel), "the little boys" (Charlie and Teddy), and Grandma. Thank you for loving me always, even when I'm at my most unlovable. Thank you, Mum and Dad, for championing me, praying for me, and believing in me. I hope I can be at least half as good a parent as you have been to me. I couldn't have got by without you. Tanita, I'm glad the traumatized sister-in-law didn't put you off marrying Ben! Thank you also to my wider family for your continued support and understanding.

To my life group: the Bishops, the Selwoods, the Muncktons, Dennis, Kate, Becky, John, and Rob. Thanks for keeping me sane, letting me cry a lot, and praying without ceasing. On a practical note, thank you also for the thousands of dinners, evenings of *Strictly* and *Downton*, doing my washing, and attempting to wear my jeans by accident. Thank you to the wider church; in particular the Evanses, Davita, and the Yeners for your time, prayer, and consistent support.

To my wider circle of friends who have always been at the end of a phone line, or in my flat cleaning and packing – Emily, Claire, Gemma, Kate, Lauren L., Jo, Vicky, Becca, and Donna – my life would be much poorer without you all. I would definitely have gone mad from 2012 to 2014 without Mrs P. and Mrs C. by my side. Your daily support was invaluable, as was your "You're going to work in London one day" assertion. Who'd have thought it?

In my not-so-new London life, thank you to Nao, Anouk, Patch, Lizzie, Corinna, Dawn, Annie, Nikki, and Stella for the endless card games and evenings of prosecco and Sports. Thank you to those at ChristChurch London, and particularly the former Covent Garden crew and Hannah, Liam, and Helen for the welcome, friendship, and acceptance.

And last but by no means least, to Phil and Naomi. I believed it existed, but didn't expect to find it. Thank you for being totally unfazed by this topic from the start, and for letting it be something we can laugh, joke, and talk about. Your love, support, and presence in my life is much more than I ever could have asked for or imagined. I love you both very much.

Contents

Introduction

Maybe you've picked this book up wanting some much-sought-after answers about how to get through this unknown and unwanted world of separation and divorce. Maybe you've decided separating is the only way forward for your marriage, but you're not completely sure what this looks like. Perhaps a well-intentioned friend has passed this book to you and suggested you read it, and you're thinking, *Great – just what I need right now – another self-help book*. And if you have the same gut reaction to those words as I once did, I would completely understand if you decide to add it to the big pile of unread books beside your bed or else put it quickly back on the shelf.

When people asked about the sort of book I was writing I would actively avoid using the label of "self-help" until they announced, "So it's a self-help book!" I'd mumble something vaguely affirmative but non-committal and we'd change the subject, especially once they started asking about the word count. There was just something about the connotations of the very word "self-help" that grated. But that, I realized, was the point. One of the reasons separation and divorce are so awful is because you are *by yourself*. That probably doesn't need emphasizing. Chances are, you've never felt more alone in your life: where there once was two, there is now one. Even if you have an incredible support network around you, and I hope you do, at the close of the day, we – those who are still in the process of separation or divorce – are still by ourselves.

But perhaps, even while those words niggle at you, you still feel alone. This separation is now your life, and you don't quite know where to begin on any sort of day-to-day task, let alone think you might come through this. The weight of emotion is crushing and doesn't seem as if it will end.

It might be your choice to be separated. It might have been a cataclysmic shock. It might have been a gradual realization that you'd drifted so far apart that there seemed to be no way back. Whether you are experiencing the turmoil of what seems to have been a happy marriage dissipating into separation and divorce, or you've taken the ultimate decision to leave your marriage, this is the place you've found yourself in. And I guess that's why you've chosen, been given, or stumbled across this book.

If you're looking for a book to tell you how much you are owed, this isn't it.

This is actually the book I wish I could have read. It is the little things and the big things, the pitfalls, the day-to-day blows, the hope. It is a life jacket that keeps you afloat because you will hopefully know you are not alone. There are thousands of us out there, yet sometimes it's impossible to utter what you're feeling and talk to anyone about it. Sometimes it's hard to find anyone that knows and gets it. While this may not be an easy read, I hope that there is comfort. You aren't the only person to feel it, though I wish you could be the last. You are not alone.

Why write this book?

I began writing about two years after the initial "moment" our marriage collapsed. I began to share my life changes, but quickly veered into writing to help and support people through this lonely time. The emotions, the practicalities, and the spiritual frustration were not something I wanted anyone else to have to navigate alone, and it was through that process that this book began to emerge.

I am passionate about seeing people come through the experiences of separation and divorce as whole as possible with a renewed determination, strength, and excitement for life. You don't have to be there now. Or even particularly want to be. But you've probably read this far because you'd quite like some help for yourself. So if my aim was to help people navigate their way through these experiences, then actually – yes – it *was* a self-help book I was writing!

But how is this going to help with the emotional, practical, and spiritual jungle you're in? Well, this book seeks to explore how we can keep going when we want to hide from the world. It asks questions to help you decide how to move forward, and helps to broaden your thinking to make those decisions effectively for you and your former spouse. It offers a variety of different strategies and ideas for coping with situations – from when you don't want to eat, to the world of the in-laws, and what about when everyone around you seems to be getting married or heading into retired bliss?

Not everyone copes in the same way, so throughout this book are stories, advice, and ideas from some wonderful people I'm privileged to call my friends. They each have a unique story about their separation and divorce: some chose to leave their marriage for various reasons; others had separation and divorce thrust upon them. Each expresses differing emotions and experiences, but all offer an authentic and honest insight into their own struggles and triumphs. Everyone has their story; no one's is the same – which is why it's impossible for someone else to tell you how to act in your marriage, and why the questions here are to help you to decide what is best for you, your marriage, your ex, and your family. My hope is that in one of our stories and experiences you will recognize glimpses of yourself and be encouraged to continue forward.

My story

I am divorced. I was married for five-and-a-half years in total; three of them happy. I got married when I was twenty-two, shortly before I graduated; separated at twenty-five; and was divorced at the age of twenty-eight.

I sometimes feel I have lived many lifetimes since the course of my marriage changed for ever. Some days marriage seems like a distant and hazy dream, like a past holiday or brief life-altering experience; other days I can conjure up the feelings as though they happened yesterday.

Following our third wedding anniversary, the relationship between my ex-husband and me became increasingly distant. I was finding work hard, but was soon to start a new job, while he had recently begun a new role within his department. I began to wonder whether he may be suffering from depression. For the next two months life became increasingly difficult, but I felt sure it would resolve itself eventually, especially if he were able to seek medical help. I can vividly recall the moment when, in late August while on holiday, I found evidence on his phone of his having a relationship with another woman. I had asked him about this previously but did not trust he was telling the truth. I felt deeply suspicious of the increasing distance between us. When I read the words, my world fell apart. I called various friends and my parents, then we travelled back to the UK together, emotionally in tatters and physically exhausted.

Over the next five months I was in turmoil, not knowing whether our marriage would work as I began my new job. After some time living with parents (him), friends (me), and then back together but in separate rooms, by Christmas of that year he had moved out, choosing not to cut ties with the woman with whom he had started a relationship. The next fourteen months were excruciatingly hard.

I prayed, we met, and made various attempts at moving forward with different levels of commitment to the cause. I desperately wanted our marriage to succeed: I had married for life. My faith was extremely important to me, and became even more so, as I learned God was a true constant in my life, around even when other people simply couldn't be. Very few people knew the details of our separation as I wanted the door to be open for him to come back relatively easily. I offered everything I possibly could, but it takes two to make a marriage work, and dragging it along simply wasn't working. After much contemplation, in February, a year-and-a-half after that initial discovery moment, I asked him to choose between divorce or committing to reconciling: he chose to divorce.

I could go into detail about what happened, but while it is my story, it is also his. For everything I say, there will be so much left unsaid. I wrestled with this for a long time. I felt I owed it to you, the reader of this book, to share my experiences. It's not because I mind talking about it now, although I used to mind. I knew that by telling my own story I would be telling my ex-husband's too. I am not perfect, nor is he. I was not the model wife, nor he the model husband. We both made mistakes, and while society could choose to judge by magnitude of mistake, or apportion blame, God spoke to me about my attitude.

In divorce, as in marriage, He told me to honour my ex-husband. When you know, as you may well do, the unutterable pain tied to divorce, this is not an easy call. It is counter-cultural, when the world would tell you to squeeze an ex-spouse for all you can get and to demand back everything you put into your marriage.

Honouring him means not holding his mistakes up to public scrutiny, in the same way I am unlikely to confess all my own errors and faults except to God. It means acknowledging the great parts of our marriage, as well as its ultimate failure. Honouring him has meant adopting the same attitude to divorce that I had in mind when making my marriage vows. If I claim to have forgiven him, how can I remain bitter? How can either of us be forgiven or released if I hold on to every detail of the past for all to see? I still have to bring my anger before God sometimes, though it has become less frequent.

It's not easy

The nuances of my experience may have striking similarities to yours or they may be entirely different. Each story has its own complications and challenges, but the experiences gained and shared are valuable nonetheless. My separation wasn't expected and I hadn't seen it coming. I was convinced – hopeful – that he was ill rather than engaging in a relationship with someone else. Divorce became the only way forward, as there was only me who wanted the marriage to work.

I was overwhelmed. One of the few things I knew was that at the end of whatever process happened, I wanted to be better rather than bitter. So this is the book I longed for – a book of help and support with the day-to-day minutiae and the enormous, seemingly impossible-to-answer questions. I wanted to know how I was supposed to keep going when all I wanted to do was hide. How did separation work? Did we still see each other? What happened next? How did I keep going? How did I do this *well* even if it didn't end "well"? What about all our wedding things? What about me?

I wanted practical ideas and help and to know I wasn't alone, but I didn't know where to begin. I felt lost and confused, because, to be honest, everything had seemed pretty OK. I had friends, family, and a support network, yet I had no idea where to go or how to continue. Every couple has times of ups and downs, but this was a whole new level. All I knew was that I didn't want a bitter divorce. I find it hard to hold a grudge anyway, but I knew that holding a grudge here wasn't going to help me. I wanted someone who *knew* and who'd been there. I wanted to find a friend who "got it" in a way that only someone who'd been there could. I was lucky: I found this friend, Ellie. But it left me thinking that there are so many others like me, like Ellie, like you, who need someone who knows. We want questions that help us to think about what to do next and strategies to help us cope until we can figure out what we're going to do. We want to know what we might expect next in a world that's full of blind-siding moments. While elements of my faith have helped me through, and therefore pepper this book in examples, you are free to follow the Bible's wisdom and any of the suggestions as you wish, and I hope you feel welcome and connected whether you are of the same faith, a different faith, or none at all. I hope you feel among friends.

This book is for those who want to do separation and divorce well, even though it might not be what they had wanted. If you hope your story will have a different ending, I'd recommend reading books on reconciliation too. But sometimes things happen that we don't expect. Sometimes we have to make decisions that feel impossible and lead us to doing things we never thought we would. This book will hopefully provide some practical insights into separating well. Perhaps for you that will mean your reconciliation is possible as you've chosen positive actions and taken consideration of your other half. Perhaps it will mean ending, or agreeing to end, your marriage through divorce. It explores how divorce doesn't have to be the end of your life, your faith, or your dreams.

It's not easy. But it *is* possible, and you are not alone.

PART ONE

What Happens Next?

Chapter One

Seeking Support

Suddenly alone

When I was very little, I firmly believed that when I became a grown-up I would morph into another person, just like a caterpillar changes into a butterfly. This person would be an adult person like those I saw around me – people who made decisions and had adult lives. They would be a version of me, but a grown-up one with the capacity to make grown-up decisions and do things like have a job and buy a house. I guess my childhood self couldn't fathom how I would ever be an adult – I couldn't make big grown-up decisions. I wouldn't be the one getting married and having babies. It wouldn't be me fulfilling childhood dreams: it would be the magical adult reincarnation of me.

I can't pinpoint the moment I realized this wasn't how life worked. It was more of a gradual understanding that this was it – that *I* was it. There was no one more "adult" who was coming along to take over. Terrifyingly, it was actually going to be up to me – and me alone.

Separation throws a curve ball. In what feels like the work of a moment, you're an adult alone. You've suddenly got to be more of an adult than you've ever been before, when you feel more like a lost child than you ever thought possible. In my entire adult life up to that point I'd always had someone alongside me, to help make the big decisions. But now I was on my own. Simple decisions like "What should I have for tea?" still needed making. Other, theoretically lovely, choices such as where to go on holiday felt mountainous and hardly worth the effort required (even if it's half an hour down the road, it's worth it – believe me). Then came the life choices. To change internet provider or to not change internet provider? Which is the best deal on car insurance? The water bill has been overpaid, underpaid, not paid at all.

And because I was still that same little person who believed that one day I'd morph into a grown-up, I gave in to my fear and became overwhelmed by the responsibility. Again, I realized – I was it. There was no one else to do this for me. Where problems had formerly been halved, now they seemed doubled.

Adulting is hard.

Shouldn't I be able to cope alone?

It's because being a grown-up is hard work that we need other people to share the burden. You may feel like you're falling apart. Even things like eating and sleeping can feel impossible. Having practical support and a physical presence can be a huge help at these times. We needn't feel guilty about taking someone else's time – something we'll explore later in this chapter. We all need help at times.

There's also a reason this chapter is first in the book – seeking out support in this situation is essential. I was, as everyone ideally is, married to my best friend. So when that best friend and I split up, I didn't just lose a husband, I lost my confidant, the one who understood me with a glance, and who could unravel an entire backstory behind a word or half-finished sentence. In many ways it is hard to comprehend that we were ever that close, because now we're strangers.

In marriage you hope to, and often do, find a friend, a lover, a companion, a helper: all of these are lost in that time when you need them most. One of the hardships of divorce, and there are many, is the loss of that companion. The irony is they are the one person you most want to talk to, and the one you are least able to. Where do you go when the principal person you spoke to about your problems is now part of them? Where do you go when the friend you'd discuss your deepest issues with is now the one causing them? Perhaps when you do talk, they don't say what your heart yearns for them to say, or they listen without hearing, leaving you feeling entirely disregarded. Where there was once understanding, intuition, and compassion, the conversation just doesn't quite fit as it used to. We have to find support and solace from others because we can no longer find it in our spouse.

Whether you like talking or want to hide under your duvet for the next three years, chances are you need support. If the idea of seeking professional help or talking to someone about the issues within your heart and marriage makes you baulk, try not to skip this section! Nothing in divorce is easy, but a shared burden can, and often does, make things easier. Separation, emotional or physical, can feel intensely lonely. I felt unloved, unwanted, and disregarded. I didn't want to have to get in touch with someone every time I felt low; I wanted them to be in touch with me. It wasn't because I thought they should always be thinking of me, but because their messaging or calling without me asking showed me I was loved. Within this chapter we are going to explore different ways to seek out, ask for, and accept support, and where that support might come from.

Think back to a time a friend needed your help, or a family member was having a crisis. Maybe you offered help or support, and put yourself out when they accepted that offer, regardless of personal inconvenience. Maybe you didn't particularly want to help when they accepted a previous offer, but you may well have done so anyway. These words from Ecclesiastes, which are often used at weddings, have such a resonance:

> *Two are better than one, because they have a*
> *good return for their labour:*
> *If either of them falls down, one can help the*
> *other up.*
> *But pity anyone who falls and has no one to*
> *help them up.*
> *Also, if two lie down together, they will keep*
> *warm. But how can one keep warm alone?*
> *Though one may be overpowered, two can*
> *defend themselves.*
> *A cord of three strands is not quickly broken.*[1]

A friend to help you up, lie down beside you, keep you safe, and help defend you is invaluable. Finding some friends to fit this bill is important, and as we'll explore, they might not be the ones you immediately consider.

I'm ashamed of my separation

I didn't tell anyone about my separation for a long time; even some of my very best friends weren't aware until a couple of months after it happened. Why? In part it was due to the sense of failure I felt that my marriage had ended. From the outside it had looked ideal; I certainly hadn't mentioned we'd had a difficult time the last couple of months. In fact I'd been expecting it to blow over; I was ashamed it hadn't. Secondly, it was hard to articulate the pain and emotional fallout to lots and lots of people, and I certainly wasn't about to explain any ins-and-outs to those who were essentially strangers yet wanted to know. I've known others who have announced what

---

1   Ecclesiastes 4:9–12.

has happened publicly on social media. These seem to be the two conflicting approaches to the situation: one extends it to everyone in their social circles; the other shuts down and keeps it secret. When divorce or separation hits our worlds, keeping it quiet or "secret" can be for good reason.

You may feel that the last thing you want to do is tell anyone what has happened in your marriage and relationship breakdown. Secrets are powerful. They can be exciting, like looking forward to a surprise party. They can also be painful, like being excluded from a playground secret. And they can also be dangerous – things we would rather no one ever knew about us. Secrecy, when it is triggered by shame, is a tiring and complex place to be. We believe that no one will love us if they knew what we've really done, or that they will judge us if they found out the truth.

I had an accurate perception that my marriage had ended in a way it was not "supposed" to. Ideally, my marriage would have ended in death – not that I'd had any murderous thoughts – but rather that is the way all life ultimately concludes, and the vow one commits to in a wedding ceremony. My shame was founded on a basis of not having achieved a goal I had committed to. It was obvious: we weren't together. I was ashamed we had not achieved what many others clearly could, especially when it came to our contemporaries. They were fine; why weren't we?

But perhaps I was asking myself the wrong question. One of those same contemporaries cried and prayed with me and expressed a "there but for the grace of God go I" sentiment. It wasn't trite but heartfelt, and it was a huge relief. I realized this could have happened to her. It could happen to anyone. As we explored in the introductory chapter, none of us is the perfect marriage partner; no one has the perfect marriage. Simply because another couple had made slightly different choices or stayed together didn't mean they somehow had it sorted. Maybe if I'd done things differently, it would have been different, but I couldn't undo the past. I could have come home from work earlier, I could have contributed more to our home, been more encouraging – any number of things. But berating myself, or feeling ashamed or that somehow I'd failed, wasn't going to change what had happened. To move through the shame I had to acknowledge what I could have done differently and forgive myself for potentially wrong decisions. I could, and even did, apologize to my ex for decisions I'd made or assumptions I'd had that weren't right. Perhaps my friends' marriage was still intact, but I didn't need to be ashamed mine was not. Theirs was hard too, whatever my Instagram-ideal picture of their life looked like.

But while feeling ashamed is not healthy, shame is hard to counteract. Do you feel that you have done something wrong, or acted selfishly? If you do, consider how to put things right instead of feeling weighed down by shame. Perhaps you need to acknowledge something you feel contributed to the breakdown of the marriage. You may also need to forgive yourself. You can beat yourself up over it, but what good will that ultimately achieve? We could *all* be better. We could all do more. We also need to release the shame of our spouse's actions. We are not responsible for their decisions; they are. Any shame attached to their decisions is theirs to work through, not for us to carry.

We may also want to keep our marital breakdown a secret because of what we ourselves have done. Bringing secrets into the open can be incredibly freeing. By sharing our secrets with a close friend, we are able to release some of the hold the secrets have over us. If we acknowledge our shame, it can no longer hold us prisoner. We no longer need to be afraid of being "found out". We shall still be deemed worthy of our friends' love and affection.

We can choose whom to talk to about fears and the weight of our perceived shame, rather than seek to hide away the facts of our separation or divorce. Taking time to process what has happened and letting people know gradually when you feel able is helpful; trying to explain the situation to everyone day after day is exhausting. But keeping what has happened a secret because you're ashamed of it means the situation keeps a hold over you and places further emotional strain and burden on you. It's a difficult tension to manage, but it is important for us to distinguish between not feeling up to talking and being ashamed of what has happened to us.

Questions to consider

Do you feel shame or embarrassment at the end of your relationship?

Do you feel your own actions contributed to the breakdown of your marriage?

Is there anything you need to ask forgiveness for, or to forgive yourself for?

Where can I find support?

With the breakdown of your relationship may come a change in the network of your friends. Sometimes the friends you become the closest to during this time are the ones you may least expect to. In my own separation, the people I told first were those who I knew would pray for us, as this was particularly important to me. The second group of people I told were not necessarily our closest friends, but the people immediately around us, whose wisdom we had benefited from in the past. They were the ones who could, and did, provide day-to-day practical help. Telling my oldest and closest friends happened much later because I knew I would need to, and want to, talk about the separation in depth with them, in all its raw emotional honesty.

Discussing separation and divorce can be emotionally exhausting, so it's fine to give yourself a break. While it may feel as if there are no other subjects in the world that are as important – which is no bad way to feel – it is also helpful to lose ourselves in menial tasks or the stories of someone else to forget our own troubles for a short time.

There are few rules or ideals on the right or wrong person to reach out to, but it is important to consider our motives if we are speaking exclusively to someone of the opposite sex. Spending time with couples can help to offer a more balanced view of circumstances and events, while spending time with other single people can help us feel positive about the future. Spending time with those who are older, and hopefully with wisdom to share, can help us see that no marriage is plain sailing. Speaking to our ex requires a new world of boundaries, as we will explore later.

First, even when we are with those closest to us, we do not have to reveal everything. The same is true for acquaintances who might want to know more! Regardless of previous closeness, their similar experiences or social invitations, there is no obligation to talk to anyone in particular. While they might wish to know where your spouse is, how you are coping, and what exactly led up to this situation, that is your business. It is not theirs. There is no requirement to engage on this topic and while it is helpful to speak to someone who's been in the situation themselves, you don't have to speak to every one of them.

When choosing who to seek support from, it may be worth considering what these different friends excel at and how they spend their time. Are they often free at the weekend? Does their family regularly sit down to dinner at a particular time? Are they a keen cook? Do they spend time out walking? Are they particularly good with DIY crises? Choosing particular friends to seek help from also alleviates the worry of burdening a small number of people. I was a regular at the dinner table of my "second family" with whom I lived for a time. I could text at the right time and just pop round for tea. In fact, I didn't even need to let them know; I knew what time tea was and if I arrived, they welcomed me in. This daily support when

I had started a new job and was struggling to manage all the day-to-day chores was a huge benefit, not to mention helping me not to give in to my desire to avoid food.

Long-term friends may be particularly helpful in offering a broad perspective on the relationship issues you've been working through. Friends who live nearby are well placed to keep an eye on you and offer practical assistance and emotional support. Friends who live further away can provide an opportunity to get away from your everyday life and go to a place where you can feel loved and be yourself. If you find many of your friends seem to have disappeared, perhaps seeking out older friendships that pre-date your relationship may bring a new lease of life and source of support. Perhaps there are friendships from university or school, or a former workplace, you can look to rekindle. After separating unexpectedly, I got back in touch with an old university friend, only to discover that she also had recently separated. These old new friendships, which can be exclusively yours, can offer a great deal of comfort.

There may be others who have also separated or divorced who you are aware of through mutual friends. I looked for new friends who could identify with my situation by asking my friends. Through my parents' church I met Ellie, who had separated from her ex-spouse about six months before me. Because of her recent experience of divorce, when I asked questions I felt they didn't come across as stupid or somehow unrealistic, and often the answer was reassuring. In time to come, you may be able to be this friend to others. Regardless of how long ago someone's divorce experience was, they can often still relate to the emotions you are experiencing, so don't be afraid to approach them. Chances are it was a hugely difficult time in their life too, and they will want to offer reassurance and positivity that this isn't the end of the journey, even though it's an uphill slope at the moment. In fact, their present situation may be a source of hope that life does not end in separation or divorce.

A huge encouragement to me was the number of people who, on discovering I was separated, told me that they too had been divorced. These came from surprising quarters: people I had known my whole life who had grown-up children, and others who had been married prior to their current marriage. In many ways, why should I have known? Your divorce, while always a part of your past, does not remain at the forefront of life for ever. A couple of years down the line, it is not always the first thing that crops up, so to hear these surprising facts about people was a huge relief. It didn't mean I necessarily told them anything about my circumstances, but it meant that when they said they understood, I knew that they fully appreciated it and truly did.

If you're finding it difficult to find anyone to confide in, or don't want to ask, I would thoroughly recommend the Restored Lives course.[2] Aimed at anyone experiencing relationship breakdown, however recently or long ago, the course is full of those in the same position as you. When I took part, and every time I have volunteered to help since, I have found liberation in speaking about what had happened, and to be in a room of people who share much of your experience can bring insight and relief. Some of their experiences are included in this book. Remember: you are not alone. You're not the only one.

Questions to consider

Make a list of friends. Who are the people you would like to speak to? Can you get in contact with them and arrange to get together?

Are there any people you do not want to share your circumstances with at this point?

---

2   Restored Lives is a course for those recovering from relationship breakdown. It is often run by churches but offers emotional and practical support regardless of belief or background. See www.restoredlives.org

Think about different "zones" of your life; for example, family, neighbours, work, faith groups, hobbies, and interests. Who are your closest friends in these areas?

Considering that list, who might you like to speak to about what has happened who might offer support?

Consider what different friends' strengths are, and how you might best ask them to help you.

Where did your biggest support come from?

Rowena: My friends. My family are not great at talking about big things. It was hard to talk to them, as they are not that emotionally "open".

Carol: My greatest support came from my friends: a Christian family that are actually closer now than my real family, and especially my church small group. I'm not sure I would have survived without them. They provided much-needed laughs and hugs when I couldn't stop the tears.

Decobe: Apart from my daily prayer and Bible reading, the biggest support came from some non-Christian close friends who really rallied round and encouraged and supported me whenever needed. These individuals proved their true friendship, unlike some in my church, which is where I would have expected it.

May: I got most support from a professional CBT therapist. My brother and sister-in-law are close but I didn't want to burden them too much with talking about how terrible things were. My close friend and prayer partner and other friends who had been through divorce were also helpful. Sadly my parents had passed away previously and my in-laws supported my ex.

Reaching out

Being alone can be horrible, whether separating was for the best or not. Even if you like time to yourself, you've been used to having someone there to turn to. Even if you do want to reach out, you may feel that you can't call on your friends *every* time you need them.

What I found really helpful were the daily texts I received from my mum and close friends. Mum would text me early every morning. It meant that by the time I arrived at work, I would have a message from her to begin my day – a lifeline. The texts I received contained Bible verses, encouragement, invitations to tea, and anecdotes from my friends' day-to-day lives. The fact that they were reaching out to me told me that I was valued and loved. That is true for you too – you are valuable and you are loved.

In the 2011 film *The Help*, Mae Mobley is a small child, generally disregarded and only wheeled out on special occasions with an unrealistic expectation of perfect behaviour. Taking care of her, in a motherly role, Mae Mobley's nanny encourages her to repeat how smart, kind, and important she is. The last two are particularly pertinent for us. We can be kind, even in the face of separation and divorce. We are important. *You are important.* Even when you don't feel like it, you are important. Sometimes we have to ask a friend to show it to us and explain that we will need to hear it every day (sometimes several times a day). Even if none of your friends have offered to do this, it is perfectly acceptable to ask. In my experience, many friends will be glad of something practical they can do. If you feel it is a burden or an imposition, perhaps ask them to text you on one specific day of the week so that you know they're thinking of you. Ask seven different friends, one for each day. Knowing you're in someone's thoughts is a powerful reminder you are loved and considered, especially at a time when it is easy to feel disregarded and unloved.

The world we live in allows us to be easily connected with others at our loneliest times. Perhaps you could look to contact friends through FaceTime or Skype. One of my friends would Skype me in the evening. We'd cook dinner together, watch TV together, and pass the time of day. Her "presence" provided the company I so craved, even while we were ninety miles apart.

It is difficult when you feel alone and your friends aren't responding to your messages, as it can compound the loneliness. For me, my faith was essential here, as believing that God was (is!) always available to talk to provided me with comfort. To be honest, this sometimes didn't compare to human companionship, which was what I craved. Distracting yourself at these points may be necessary, and it's something we'll explore later in this section.

Questions to consider

Could you ask some friends to text on particular days of the week or at particular times of the day you know you are going to find challenging?

What is your preferred method of communication?

Can you FaceTime or Skype with friends?

Losing friends

A particularly painful part of marital breakdown is the friendships and other relationships that can splinter too. There may be some friends that were naturally more "yours" or "theirs", but if you have been together for some time, or if you are friends with couples, which friendship then wins out?

It is a thorny area, where there is potential for feelings of rejection, hurt, and abandonment. For couples to maintain friendships with both of you and avoid one of you feeling "blamed" for the split, or sidelined, can be difficult. It is not our responsibility to make these decisions for our friends. Their choices are their own responsibility, but we can also take responsibility for how we behave in this time.

The way we approach our shared friendships is important – it is not a competition to win the most friends, much as it is not a competition to keep the most "stuff". If your aim is to somehow get back at your ex by telling everyone all the bad things they did, it is unlikely to be the cathartic experience hoped for and may damage your relationships in the process. While we don't have to lie about our feelings, behaving with decorum will result in stronger friendships over all. We can be honest and frank without expecting our friends to feel the way we do.

Our friends will also be experiencing their own difficulties in this situation: who do they support? How do they support one or both of you well? How much of what they are being told from either side is true? They may also be hurt, surprised, and saddened that your marriage has broken down and by the actions different parties have taken. This doesn't mean they don't like you. It does mean they too may need time to think about what has happened. Just because they do not support your side of the story straight away does not mean they're not your friend. Good friends also challenge us when supporting us. Understanding that they are also processing loss, albeit in a different way, helps us to reduce our expectation that they will fully support every single thing we say.

So retreating from certain friendships may feel necessary. It might be that you want to talk to these friends and ask them to seek out a deeper relationship with your ex to support them, particularly if you still care for your ex. Explaining why you feel it is sadly no longer appropriate for you to seek out their support may be necessary. It isn't that you don't like them but giving your ex the opportunity to experience support is important too. It is a fact of life that friendships can be seasonal but this doesn't diminish the pain of losing them. Of course, you may not feel saddened to lose some friendships! This is also absolutely acceptable. Fading out of someone's life through the experience of a relationship breakdown is just what happens sometimes. My suggestion would be to end the relationship well: try not to burn bridges or put people down. You may meet again one day, and even if not, hopefully you will not regret the way you behaved, but rather be proud of your kind conduct at such a difficult time.

There are other friendships that may suddenly disappear from you. Many of those you thought of as friends have "sided" with your ex. This feels enormously unfair. They haven't heard your side of the break up, they've not sought you out to support you. It is an incredibly painful experience, compounded as it is by your separation. As we find on the playground, we can't force people to be friends with us and in this situation it's agonizing. It is easy to be angry with these so-called friends for the hurt they have caused us, so let us consider it from their viewpoint. These friends may have external forces acting on their choices: other friendships where your spouse is a central part, or a spouse or partner who is influencing them. Other friends may seem to disappear spurred on by a desire to be neutral, thereby offering support to neither partner. While this avoids the appearance of taking sides, it can also feel like abandonment. Others may not know quite what to say to you: it's not that they don't care, but they aren't sure how to express their emotion and don't know whether to sympathize, console, or celebrate. Instead, they say nothing out of fear of hurting or offending you; yet to the one suffering, it can feel like a further betrayal and abandonment. Even so, if you feel brave enough, gently asking them why they've not been in touch could be an option. This may enable them to honestly say they haven't known what to do or say.

Managing our pain and emotions around this is extremely difficult, exacerbated as it is by the rejection, hurt, and pain we are already experiencing. It is worth considering why our friends have felt unable to support us, and to forgive them for the pain caused, whether unintentionally or deliberately. Grieving these friendships is also important.

Questions to consider

Are there particular friends you or your ex-spouse are particularly close to? Perhaps make a list and highlight these in different colours.

With this in mind, are there any friendships you feel you need to let go of?

Are there any friendships you feel sad to have lost in this time? Is there a way to re-establish contact?

Are there friends you want to contact as your lives potentially drift apart? Can you end the friendships positively and with thanks for their presence in your life?

Are there friendships that have soured that you want to end well? Perhaps write a short letter, thanking them honestly for any support or good times spent together.

Asking for and accepting help

One night, less than a week into the "new normal" of post-cataclysmic break-up conversation, I had reached a point where I couldn't cope any longer. I wasn't suicidal, but the prospect of crying into my pillow again, and not knowing what on earth to do was too much.

I knew the leaders of my church were not those who were early to bed; in fact, I was in awe of my friend's ability to be fully functioning despite having been up folding laundry at 1 a.m.

Knowing this, at gone midnight I decided to drive over. If their light was on, I reasoned, I would go and knock on the door. If it wasn't, I'd just go home again. I pulled up, parked up, and was grateful to see their lights still blazing. I knocked on the door. They invited me in, listened to me and prayed with me, despite the lateness of the hour. I'd not revealed a hint of our marital difficulties until now, so for them this was a bolt from the blue at one in the morning.

Despite the lateness of the hour, I hadn't known what else to do. I couldn't manage the emotions and confusion alone, and those feelings outweighed the guilt I felt at interrupting their night. I also knew deep down that if I ever told them I had nearly visited they would cry, "Well, you should've come and knocked! Even if the lights weren't on!"

One of my close friends gave me the spare key to their house. If they woke up to find me on the sofa in the morning, they were OK with that. I moved into their house for an extended stay, unable to live in a broken marital home any longer.

I much prefer to give time and help to others rather than ask for help. In fact, I need to be more selective in the time I give away, but I rarely offer help without being sincere. You may want to help anyone in need, or you may feel you would only want to give of your time and resources to those who are closest to you. Think back to the last time you offered someone help. They may have taken you up on that offer at a horribly inconvenient time, when you'd forgotten all about it. But you worked with it and made it work because they are your friend. And it's the same for you. When people are offering help, take it. Accept the offer of dinner. Call people at inconvenient hours because they've said you can. Stay over, so you've got a friendly face to wake up to on that difficult day of the year. Accepting offers of help is easier than asking for them. But don't let that put you off – the chances are that those who love you are wondering how they can best help you.

Giving friends some options and ideas of how to help means they can choose what works for them. Perhaps you need a meal, or a little break away. Maybe you need help with a household chore or childcare. You might need someone to text you next Thursday because it would've been a particular anniversary. Make it clear to friends that they don't need to do all that is asked of them; they may even know others willing to help. In any case, never be afraid to ask. The relief friends feel at being able to help is helpful to them in turn.

Accepting these offers of help was the first step along a road to deepening friendships that are now constants in my life. We weren't made to live in isolation; you'll work out a way to repay the favours later, so accept help when you need it.

Questions to consider

What would be the best offer of help you could receive right now? Make a list of particular things that would make a difference to your life.

Do you know someone who would be able to provide help in these areas? Think back to the list you made earlier about different friends. Does anyone particularly come to mind?

Have you received any offers of help or support recently? Choose at least one to graciously accept.

Being afraid to ask too much

Asking for and even accepting offers of help can sometimes lead to guilt. I have a tendency to carry guilt around like a handbag. It goes everywhere with me, weighing me down unnecessarily. I've carried guilt around for so long that I don't even notice I've got it. I feel guilty about a lot of things: accepting help, asking a question, leaving somewhere to go home – pretty much anything really. Much like Mary Poppins' bag, I can pull anything out of my guilt complex.

But guilt is a particularly unproductive emotion – I "feel bad", overanalyse my decisions and end up in a quandary over what to do. The guilt doesn't then help my decision because generally the decision that makes me feel guilty is the right one, so even though I make the right decision, I feel guilty – how's that for a complex?

So why do I feel guilty? It's not usually because I have done anything inherently terrible. I'm fairly well behaved, though by no means perfect, but a large part of it comes from a well-intentioned desire to please people, and also through an oft-misplaced sense of what I "should" and "shouldn't" do. I don't want to put people out or make them go out of their way for me, so I sometimes feel guilty in accepting help. I feel bad over leaving somewhere, even though my time is mine to allot. I feel bad for spending time with my family, bad for spending time with friends, bad for spending it by myself. Whatever I do, I can end up feeling guilty.

What I have come to realize, is that if I have done something actually wrong, what I tend to feel is conviction. Conviction is that inner voice – a little Jiminy Cricket conscience – when you become or are made aware of your sinfulness, or guilt. A conviction is something to be listened to, a reminder of what your behaviour should be and that it's time to change. There's nothing wrong with being convicted in the internal sense; it is a reminder to assess what you have done and put it right: a helpful, if very uncomfortable, thing. A guilt complex holds you back because you feel bad, while conviction can push you forward into improvement.

Are you toting around a guilt complex, or are you feeling genuinely convicted? If it's the former, leave it at home. Step out of the house without it and feel liberated. Work out when you take it with you. Do you always take it to the same issues? If it's the latter, listen up! I don't believe anyone was put on this earth to feel permanently guilty. Sometimes this means we need to face up to our decisions and mistakes, me included. Condemnation is a horrible thing to live under, whether it's from someone else, or you condemning yourself. By holding on to guilt, we condemn ourselves to misery. A big difference between a conviction and a guilt complex is that conviction should inspire change, whereas the complex wants you to wallow in unnecessary guilt.

I still didn't want to put people out, but I decided to accept their offers of help. Other people's perceptions of what I was doing began to take second place – if I have good reasons for a decision then that should be enough for me. I stopped condemning myself for letting others help me. I found this Bible story particularly helpful:

> *Jesus bent down and wrote with his finger*
> *in the dirt. They kept at him, badgering him.*
> *He straightened up and said, "The sinless*
> *one among you, go first: Throw the stone."*
> *Bending down again, he wrote some more in*
> *the dirt.*
>
> *Hearing that, they walked away, one after*
> *another, beginning with the oldest. The*
> *woman was left alone. Jesus stood up and*
> *spoke to her. "Woman, where are they? Does*
> *no one condemn you?"*
>
> *"No one, Master." "Neither do I," said Jesus.*
> *"Go on your way. From now on, don't sin."[3]*

No one was sin-free and therefore they couldn't condemn anyone else. All the condemnation was lifted from that woman – I can

---

3   John 8:6–11, MSG.

imagine the relief. If people are judging us, let them. Their lives will not be perfect. We can take responsibility for wrong actions, but we are also responsible for releasing ourselves from the "should" and "ought tos" in our lives.

Questions to consider

Are there any actions you feel guilty about that you feel contributed to your separation or divorce?

Was that behaviour wrong? Do you need to ask for forgiveness?

What are the areas of guilt in your life? Have you actually done anything "wrong" in these areas or are these "should" and "ought tos"?

Managing other people's emotions

Managing our own emotions can take up all our energy, and later in this section we explore both how to switch off from and engage with this. But when anything happens in a person's life, others react to it. When this is a positive change, it is easier to handle others' emotions; any negativity can be absorbed by our own joy at the situation. When it is a negative change, it can become harder to manage other people's expectations and emotions about what has happened.

When a divorce or break-up happens, many people will have an opinion. The majority will have heard one side of the story that led to the situation; the kinder ones will remember this and bear it in mind as they hear. Others will want to tell us their perspectives on the situation or people involved and this is often hard to listen to and process in amongst our own emotional turmoil. Some of the hardest conversations I had were reacting to other people's emotions projected on to me:

"You must be heartbroken"

Actually, right now, I'm not – but do ask me again in a few hours' time.

Emotions can change quickly, and while one moment can have us feeling relieved it's all over, the next can have us crying in a heap in the corner. Assuming someone else's emotions is unhelpful. Perhaps try a response such as "I have a lot of different emotions, which I won't go into now, but right now I'm doing all right. Thank you for being considerate of how I might be feeling." It's good to acknowledge that they care (even if we feel they're digging for us to pour out our soul to them) but that our emotions aren't necessarily always at a low – sometimes we do feel an internal thankfulness or relief. We don't have to share that, but letting them know we're not a permanent crying mess is okay, even if that is the scenario 99 per cent of the time.

"Well, it's good that's over!"

Er, no it's not. I never wanted it to be over. I get what you mean – it is now done and dusted – but no, it's not good.

I heard this statement said once my divorce was finalized. I understood the sentiment; it was well intentioned. The person was glad I could move on in some sense. I, having never wanted a divorce, was not happy it was over, even though I was glad there was resolution. My response went something along the lines of, "It is helpful that there is a conclusion, yes, though I still feel sad that it has ended this way." This helped me to acknowledge the truth of the sentiment, while allaying the assumption that it was a positive step in my life. Responses that give credence, where appropriate, to the person's statement and then add in a "but" or "although" help to save face for the other person by not directly contradicting them, yet setting their perspective straighter in line with what we are really feeling. Of course, you may want to say "Yes! Thank goodness!" – and that's fine too!

"I never liked him/her anyway"

There are a couple of reasons for this particular reaction. Chances are, they actually never did like them – in which case you may well have already known that and this situation has merely exacerbated that emotion. Or, in more cases, they're aware your ex has hurt you and now your friend wants to seek to protect you as much as they can.

The difficulty with this statement is that expressing dislike towards your ex does not help bring you to a healthy or helpful place. If you have children, you will need to maintain the relationship with your ex-spouse in as positive a way as possible, and if you don't have children you will ideally want to work to as amicable and smooth a solution as possible.

We get the essence of what they're saying of course: yes, they may have been a total tool. Yes, I am totally amazing and they should have realized what they'd be missing. But I married them. At one stage I clearly thought there was something pretty phenomenal about them. I don't think of them in that same way now, but there are many, many shades of grey in between "perfect" and "total idiot". Listing things that are bad about them is actually likely to make me like the person listing them less.

Trying to express this is difficult, particularly if your ex hurt you badly and you have not yet felt able to forgive them; in many ways you may fully agree with your friend! Try a response such as, "They have behaved badly, I'm not disputing that, but obviously there were many things I did like about them otherwise I wouldn't have married them, so I'm trying not to think about it in such black and white terms."

"I thought you would be together for ever"

So did I.

To others looking in from the outside, your marriage may have appeared ideal. Shared values and dreams and a life seemingly "sorted". This is a myth in general – but when your marriage breaks down, and this was others' perception of it, there is also a lot for them to process in terms of what they thought marriage looked like and how it works. Their expression of this to you may give you opportunity to share the sadness that the break-up has caused. However, it may feel too much for you to have their sadness added to your own. If that is the case, it is perfectly permissible to say so. A sentence like "Thank you for sharing my grief at what's happened, but I find it too hard to cope with others' sadness about this too – are you able to find someone else to support you in expressing it?" may be helpful. Conversely, you may find it helpful to have someone with whom to share that sadness.

It is also good to consider that they saw your marriage as a positive, healthy relationship. If you felt you were happy for part of your marriage it is encouraging to note that others saw this as the case too. Your marriage and your happiness wasn't a lie.

The trouble is, we cannot avoid everyone, much as we might want to. It is very difficult to hide significant life changes: marriage, divorce, pregnancy, moving house. Others may be involved and you will need their support. As we go along in life, we find power in vulnerability and honesty. Acknowledging things that are hard, upsetting, and complicated with great honesty helps to allay the assumption that other people have it sorted – because no one does.

How did other people react to the news that you were separating/divorcing? How did you find this?

Carol: Most of my friends were glad and said, "About time!" I found friends from my church were more sympathetic and more understanding of the complex issues surrounding faith and divorce, though I think they mostly thought it was about time too. I wasn't really surprised with their reactions.

Decobe: Most people seemed surprised when they heard we were separating/divorcing. Although a couple of close friends weren't so surprised by the news, I found this to be more upsetting than anything else.

May: Some people wanted to offer lots of advice about legal things, of which they had no knowledge, and I would just say, "Please let's not talk about it, I want to relax." They meant well but were completely ignorant of the law. I'd say I would get advice from my solicitor. Some people prayed for us to stay together; some were sad but understood if they knew the whole story. Some don't talk to me any more but we weren't that close before. The vicars in my church were understanding, as I had come into the church to seek help when I was initially so shocked at what my ex was doing. They knew what had happened. Now some people are friends with both of us a year after we were divorced, and I even invited my ex and some mutual friends round to dinner once.

Rowena: I think my parents found it incredibly hard as they had invested so much into getting to know and welcoming my husband into our family and it really hurt them too. think they found it hard to admit to other people that it was happening. My friends were supportive.

Seeking professional help

I was acutely aware that my main topic in conversation was my separation. Feeling guilty (of course!) about boring my friends over the continual angst and anguish of my heart, I decided counselling was worth investing in. I would just pay someone to listen. People would have happily listened for free, and did, but I felt more able to talk at length, and agonize over my own problems, when I was paying someone to listen to what I had to say.

Seeking professional help can feel as daunting as asking friends for help, but in a similar way the first step on that journey is often the hardest. If you are finding divorce and separation difficult – which is not unusual – it may be that you want to seek medical or professional help. In the UK there are many options available, possibly through the NHS (National Health Service), through work, or through independent organizations. Some options you might explore are:

- *individual counselling*
- *marital counselling*
- *GP/doctor or*
- *mediation*

Of course, there is intense sadness at the end of a relationship, but feel of numb or feeling that the world would be better off without you is a signal that you need more particular help. Depression is more than sadness: it's hard to feel anything at all, even though you might want to. If this is the case for you, or even if you feel your symptoms are not so extreme, consider seeing your doctor to explore options or just to highlight that you may need support in the future. The doctor may be able to offer more targeted help. Asking friends for a recommendation, if they have had similar health issues, is particularly helpful as you know you will get a friendly, understanding listener.

As you seek this professional help, one of the hardest things may be to open up and explain what you are feeling, which is especially difficult if you're not entirely sure. Now I do love to talk, and I am usually an external processor, making sense of my emotions and feelings through discussion. But talking and opening up to someone you don't know about some very deeply felt personal pain is not easy – even when you like talking as much as I do.

A common misconception is that counselling is only about talking – and yes, in part, it is. But it's also so much more than that: insightful questions, exploring new ways of looking at a situation, and revealing issues you may not have previously considered are a few other aspects.

Speaking to my doctor also helped me to consider other options: there was the potential to be signed off work if at any point I felt everything was becoming too much for me to manage without risking my physical or mental health. Knowing this was an option somehow helped me to keep going: there was a back-up plan.

Where possible, and if you feel comfortable doing so, speaking to your manager at work may mean you are able to access free help through any health and wellbeing services in your workplace.

As I mentioned, after my separation, I decided to get counselling. This wasn't the first time I had chosen this option: I had also worked through the death of a close relative and coping with a sense of failure around my studies. It had clearly helped, as the sense of failure was nowhere near as acute as it might have been when my marriage failed – although, believe me, it was still there (and, I find, still crops up today!) This time I decided to get counselling for a few reasons:

- *I wanted to emerge from this time in my life better able to cope.*

- *I wanted to see a way forward and to work through the many issues that were cropping up.*
- *I didn't want to bore all my friends all the time with all my problems.*

Counselling can be expensive, but there are also some fantastic organizations that offer free sessions, or a "pay what you can afford" service, or are available, in the UK, through an NHS referral.

While you may be paying a counsellor to listen, you both still have to invest the time to make the relationship work. This is a good reason to give professional help a few sessions before making a decision about whether to continue. As we got to know one another a little more, I was able to open up to my counsellor. In marital counselling, in much the same way, you both need to build a relationship with the counsellor, while simultaneously working on your relationship with one another. If one of you feels particularly uncomfortable with the counsellor, do consider honouring your spouse or partner's wishes and instead finding a person with whom you both feel able to open up. If you find your doctor is not hearing what you are saying, there is no reason you should not go to another doctor in the practice, or change practice altogether, especially if the alternative comes with a good recommendation from a friend.

With counselling, you get as much out as you put in. A good counsellor will encourage you to think about new questions and ways of looking at situations. They can challenge assumptions and worldviews you didn't realize you held. They can give you strategies for thinking about and approaching emotions and situations that you might otherwise not have been able to process.

There is often a fear that a counsellor will judge you, but that's not been the case in my experience. A counsellor might challenge you on why you made a particular choice, but this is to encourage you to think it through, rather than condemn you. You will probably feel quite, or even very, exposed, but then working through difficult emotions with a trained professional is always better than turning to social media in the early hours. If you do feel judged you can always seek out a different counsellor. We don't all get on with everyone, and this is just as true in the area of professional help.

Whatever your reasons, seeking professional help is more likely to help than not. You don't have to be an eloquent speaker: just open up about one thing you don't mind talking about so much and see where the conversation takes you and what support you can be given.

Questions to consider

What are the reasons you might consider professional help?

Are you feeling numb and having difficulty feeling emotions? If so, please do contact your doctor.

How did you feel about seeking professional help?

Carol: I was happy to seek counselling prior to deciding to divorce to see if it would help us to a different outcome. Afterwards, I didn't see the point: the situation was as it was and I just had to get on with it.

Decobe: I never sought any professional help. Looking back now at those days I'm surprised how I actually made it through. I have emotional scars from this time which have affected me through the years since, but I am a lot stronger for having come through the experiences.

Rowena: We tried marriage counselling but the timing was

bad. The first Gulf War started and my husband had to go away. The counsellor said it wasn't a good time to delve into deep emotional stuff when there was so much else to deal with – meaning the men were dealing with the fact they might potentially be killed.

May: For me, seeking professional help was a bit like having a life coach; I talked about work issues and my goals there as well, as I wanted to move on and not let things hold me back.

As John Donne so succinctly put it: "No man is an island". We were not made to function alone. Having systems of support will help us with all the experiences we will have throughout this time, and no doubt far into the future. The systems and support that might suit us won't all look the same, so begin to consider where you can start to seek support.

Chapter Two

When it's Hard to...

Function

Maslow's hierarchy of needs model (shown opposite) illustrates the most basic things humans need to survive and function.[4] At the very bottom level there's the absolute essentials: air, water, food, shelter, sleep, and clothing. But when we're separated or divorcing and reeling from the aftermath of a situation we weren't expecting, eating, sleeping, and keeping going can seem like the most trivial things. Why bother? The bottom has fallen out of your world. Yet impossible as it seems, life does somehow continue and so we need to somehow engineer ourselves into the best space possible to face it.

This list of "basics" can feel overwhelming when we've been left to deal with them ourselves. There is nothing straightforward about eating when your appetite has disappeared. If someone else regularly cooked for you, or you for them, the sudden shift in dynamic can alter how you feel about eating. Sleeping becomes a challenge if someone else used to share your bed, or now despite being beside you, they feel miles away. Life continues on regardless of your personal circumstances. Getting out of bed, putting one foot in front of another – where do we begin, and why do we bother?

---

4   S. A. McLeod, 21 May 2018, *Maslow's hierarchy of needs*, retrieved from www.simplypsychology.org/maslow.html

Beginning to manage your basic needs in a straightforward, simple way can help a great deal with your emotions and perspective on separation and divorce. OK, it's not going to make the situation go away, but without meeting your basic needs, the remainder of the pyramid becomes unavailable to you. We want to have friendships, self-esteem, and to feel whole and ourselves once again. Working out what we need to survive helps us work toward these goals that, as yet, may feel difficult to achieve. This chapter offers strategies and ideas for approaching some of these basic life needs from where you actually are, while shelter and where to live are explored fully in Part Two. Here we consider the need to sleep and eat, how we exist at home alone, and how we venture out into the outside world, when all these things seem impossibly hard.

Self-actualization
desire to become the most that one can be

Esteem
respect, self-esteem, status, recognition, strength, freedom

Love and belonging
friendship, intimacy, family, sense of connection

Safety needs
personal, security, employment, resources, health, property

Physiological needs
air, water, food, shelter, sleep, clothing, reproduction

Sleep

Sleep is often hard to come by when your mind is working in overdrive, trying to puzzle out what happens next, trying to make sense of your situation. Sleep is our body's way of processing our thoughts and emotions through our subconscious... and it's essential.

> *Results from neuroimaging studies suggest that sleep loss affects the processing of emotion, with similar effects found with positive and negative stimuli. These results are suggestive of both increased reactivity, and altered connectivity. Sleep loss also seems to amplify anticipatory activity, towards all cues or when expecting negative emotional stimuli, and this discrepancy could depend on the measure of emotion... and/or task.[5]*

Sleep loss can have a negative impact on our anticipation of events and how we react to them: we expect them to be worse and that can be deeply unhelpful. For this reason, things always look slightly better – or at least more manageable – after a good night's sleep. During separation, the likelihood of disturbed sleep increases and our ability to cope with negative emotions is reduced. If you are suffering from a lack of sleep, it is prudent to delay any major decisions you may have to make, if possible, as you will likely not be thinking clearly. You could limit your decision making to a specific time of day, to ease the pressure. When a quick decision is required, it may help to turn to family or friends. If you are likely to be bothered by calls or messages, try turning your phone off or switching it to airplane mode. You could always keep a cheap back-up phone for your closest family and friends to contact you. Specifying a time frame within which you will respond to your ex can also be helpful. Set clear boundaries, so that you can seek the rest you will need.

Even putting these measures in place, however, does not guarantee a good night's sleep. I remember my bed feeling so empty and sleep

---

5   L. Beattie et al., "Social interactions, emotion and sleep" in Sleep Medicine Reviews, 24 (2015), 83–100. See www.smrv-journal.com/article/S1087-0792(14)00157-9/pdf

was sometimes a long time in coming. As I hoped my separation would be temporary, I would often stack pillows up along one side of the bed. The barrier of pillows was comforting, creating a single-sized bed and a person-sized barrier beside me. I even got out my beloved childhood doll, although sadly it didn't have that same comfort factor and I quickly put it away again. After my grandad's death, my grandma invested in a new single bed. This strategy eased the feeling of someone being missing from the space. In the case of permanent separation a new bed can help reclaim the space as your own.

It may be that a new bedtime routine is helpful. You may have gone to bed at the same time as your partner or had a routine where you worked around one another as you got ready for bed. To help develop a new normal and perhaps "trick" your body and mind, could you change the order in which you do things as part of your winding down process? Would it be helpful to have a podcast or radio show on as company while you prepare for bedtime?

It is worth considering how you feel about the space in which you sleep too. Are there any constant reminders and if so, do you like having them there? Is there a way that you can rearrange the room or furniture so that it becomes a space that is a safe haven for you at the end of a tiring day? You could consider sleeping in a different room for a while, or even just changing the orientation of the bed. I found having my ex-husband's belongings around in the bedroom particularly unhelpful, so I removed them.

I found that white noise apps (my favourite being the many different sorts of rain sounds available) helped to switch my mind off. I would read if I couldn't sleep – I wasn't disturbing anyone by having the light on. Scrolling through social media certainly wasn't a help, so building in a cut-off time for that proved useful (though challenging to commit to!)

Questions to consider

What do you find the most difficult about bedtime? Are you falling asleep on the sofa or putting off going to bed?

Write down your usual bedtime routine. How could you change two or three things to make it feel new?

Would changing the location or configuration of where you sleep help you to sleep better? Would it be easier to sleep in your guest bedroom or move your current room around slightly?

Could you purchase some new bedding or a picture to hang on the wall to feel ownership of the space?

What was the biggest challenge of day-to-day life and how did you approach it?

Decobe: Eating was a big problem for me: I just didn't want food or couldn't be bothered with preparing anything. The physical need for food was not really there any more. I had taken on a mortgage with extremely high repayments that I could ill afford, so I had to cut back to spending an absolute minimum, which also meant depriving myself of numerous meals. Silly, as I now realize, but that was the financial situation for me at that time. There was many a day when I just didn't want to get out of my bed, but I always managed to force myself to get up and get on with whatever I had to do that day. I had to keep myself busy so as not to dwell on the "finality of my marriage". This was difficult to do, as deep down I just wanted out of life. I was determined not to give in to self-pity so I threw myself into helping a close friend who was working in a touring exhibition. I got to visit Belgium, France, and Germany regularly. These were happy times while away from the home situation. Another one of my distractions was to dig up the rear garden of my home and redesign it, complete with a large wildlife pond, which still brings me a lot of pleasure each day.

Rowena: My levels of concentration were appalling. I was doing some temp work at the time and how they kept me on, I'll never know. Everyday life was complicated. I moved back to live in the same flat even though he didn't want me to, but we led separate lives as far as was possible in the army community. I think there was quite a lot of alcohol consumption involved, with lots of social nights! He then went away on active service for six months and I got a job working for the army again, covering roles where soldiers were away. Life carried on and I really enjoyed where I worked. I had good friends around me, which helped.

Carol: I don't eat when emotionally upset so the first time we separated it was good to be living with friends, as they cooked meals so I wouldn't skip them. The second time, when we actually divorced, I wasn't as upset, and I found I was eating through boredom and loneliness so the weight went on. The biggest challenge was having two businesses together and one being a franchise. I was keeping head office from finding out how unreliable he was, but eventually I had to tell them, as he smashed up my work laptop in a drunken rage. It was embarrassing as I felt this shouldn't have happened, as I am an intelligent woman! I just kept on keeping on – getting up each day and doing what needed to be done… what else could I do?

Ellie: A rather surprising challenge for me was food – it was the first time in my life I lost interest in it. It wasn't intentional; I just didn't think about it. My family nagged me so I tried to remember to eat. What really helped was friends inviting me out for dinner – I seemed to be able to eat without noticing when I was engaged in conversation. Another challenge was practical jobs around the house. For a while I begrudged the fact he wasn't there any more and I felt he should be! However, I recruited some friends who I think felt sorry for me. They fixed a few things and finished jobs he hadn't got round to doing.

May: The biggest challenge was having to live in the same house, which my solicitor advised, as it would have been too expensive to move out totally and rent somewhere. So I would occasionally stay with friends or relatives at weekends, house-sit for people and sometimes rent a room a few nights a week closer to my workplace.

Eat

If you're anything like me, or the some of the folk above, your appetite is easily affected by emotions. To me, eating is always an enjoyable, social activity. When I was little, my family all ate together at the table; good food and good conversation are synonymous to me. Cooking, however, is a necessity, and often a chore, although I quite like baking. I don't mind cooking for others, but I find putting flavours together a challenge, and not an inspiring one at that: I'd definitely be out in the first round of the cookery show *Masterchef*. Eating is significantly easier when it's with friends and I haven't had to cook the food myself! With all these elements combined, cooking for and eating by myself can be a thankless chore rather than a pleasant experience: it lacks any social element and the experience of cooking is often unsatisfying, even if the food is good. When I am miserable I lose my appetite. For a person who can graze all day, it was quite a surprise to find my appetite had vanished.

Perhaps your experience is very different. My brother – a former chef (how are we related?) – takes great joy in bringing flavours together. He finds it soothing, enjoyable, and worthwhile, and the end product is inevitably delicious. Eating may be a comfort to you or something that has comforted you throughout your life. Unhappiness seems to me to have three potential impacts on eating:

1. The person eats more than they need to.

2. The person eats much less than they need to.

3. The person becomes an incredible cook.

Being separated can have a big impact on mealtimes as they are often times of day when people sit down together. Sitting down to eat alone may hold no appeal. You may want to eat plentifully as a form of comfort. You may avoid eating altogether. Perhaps your choice of food radically changes. The more aware we are of our relationship with food, the more effectively we can put strategies in place to help us maintain a stable food relationship throughout this period.

Questions to consider

Do you want to eat more or less when you're experiencing sad or difficult times?

What would you describe as your "comfort food"?

How do you view eating – as a necessity or a pleasure? List different scenarios where this opinion changes; consider your whole life and greatest food experiences.

How do you view cooking or baking?

Our view of ourselves can often alter depending on what we eat and if we enter into a cycle of blame or guilt relating to food. Words such as "should", "ought to", and "mustn't" become natural precursors to "eat", yet result in a sense of failure as soon as we eat, or don't eat. To maintain and to aim for nutritional balance it is important to eat in moderation. It's understandable that food can be comforting at a time like this. A good strategy to help you eat in moderation is to put aside some of the food you cook. If you've always cooked for two or more then it's often easier to continue to do this. Having a freezer full of prepared meals means it's easier to eat when you need to and limit yourself to a single portion. It took me about three years to do this well, and for it not to feel like an upsetting thing to do. For some reason it made me feel more alone, so while this wasn't the best solution for me, it may well be worth you giving it a try.

Something else that can help is inviting a friend over for a meal. This draws the focus away from the food itself and turns a meal into a social occasion.

Questions to consider

If you are finding it difficult to eat in moderation consider these questions:

What foods am I most likely to eat?

What times of day am I likely to comfort eat?

Once you have an increased awareness, it becomes more possible to change the pattern. Not having the food within the home means it's obviously more difficult to eat it, so not adding it to your shopping list is a great way to begin, or even reducing the quantities you are tempted to buy. If, for example, your comfort food is crisps, allow yourself to buy one small individual packet so that there is the enjoyment of the food without the feeling of punishment from going cold turkey. It's also helpful to find something to physically do with your hands. It's hard to eat while you're knitting, playing on the PlayStation, typing, sewing, gardening. Do remember to acknowledge and reward yourself for any changes you make, no matter how small. Also, *allow* yourself to make mistakes, we all make them. You are deserving of your own kindness.

Healthy convenience foods can be a great way to build some balance into your diet: pre-chopped fruit and vegetables are readily available. Frozen fruit and veg means there's less danger of food being wasted and going off in the fridge, and it is handily there whenever you want it. Choosing to eat the healthier options over unhealthier ones helps us feel positive because *we made that choice*. Congratulating yourself on a good choice is a good feeling.

Perhaps there are certain times when you find it easier to eat more healthily. I found that lunchtime was a great time to eat salads and soups packed full of vegetables, as in the evening all I wanted was a good deal of carbs or a takeaway. During the day I would eat at work with colleagues, therefore I was less focused on the actual food and more on the social activity. This strategy helped to assuage guilt, as I knew if I'd eaten relatively healthily at lunchtime, I was at least taking care of myself in some way. I found it helpful to buy my lunches, usually a pre-made salad, to keep me eating healthily. I built it into my routine and stopped at the supermarket on the way to work each day.

Questions to consider

When could you snack healthily?

When is it more straightforward to eat fruit and vegetables?

When are the times of day you want particular foods?

But perhaps your problem is that you don't want to eat – so how do we manage a lost appetite? Fundamentally, it is important to eat, so if you're finding your appetite has entirely disappeared, it is better to just eat anyway. Eat unhealthily if you need to – but do eat. I ate takeaways with alarming regularity and at great expense. The entire five-pack of doughnuts? Yep! Healthy food will help you feel better in yourself, but if you're not eating, that's a secondary concern. First it's important just to eat.

Takeaways are helpful because of their convenience. If I felt obliged to eat, I wasn't about to be cooking as well – that was more energy than I had the capacity for. Cooking a meal for one is hard, particularly when you're used to cooking for two or more. Buying food in cut out the need for me to cook, while fulfilling my basic need for food. Gradually, as I felt more able to cope with being organized ahead of time, I found that freezer meals were a great help, and considerably less expensive than a takeaway. Admittedly, these meals may not have been much healthier, but they were cheaper and didn't have the same "guilt" attachment as ordering in. There was also little washing up to do, which in a dishwasher-less household was invaluable (keeping up with the cleaning was something I wasn't mastering on top of work and staying alive). Buying ready meals may also be a good strategy if your ex-spouse was the principal cook in your home. You do not have to become the next Gordon Ramsay (although you may feel as sweary); all you need to do is eat.

A third way to eat conveniently is to find some friends who are happy to lay an extra place at the table. You may need to find those wonderful people you can text and say, "I can't bring myself to cook and I don't want to eat. Please can I come and have tea at yours?" It's not lazy, it's honest. Food is better with friends: it's easier to eat when you're with others. Chances are they love you enough to prefer to cook you tea than have you go hungry. This was my salvation in terms of food. Whenever I couldn't bear to eat, or I knew I would just go home and not bother, I invited myself over to a friend's. I often felt guilty in doing so, but every time I was reassured that feeding one more really didn't make much difference to them – yet it made the world of difference to me. As I have said, friends and family are often glad of a practical way to help you in a difficult time, so try and say yes to help, or reach out with the suggestion if they ask whether there's anything they can do. You could persuade a friend out for a regular catch-up dinner. My friend Claire and I would meet often at the affectionately renamed "Carb Central". This gave us the time to talk things over, for me to hear about her life too, and to enjoy food in my favourite way: cooked by and eating with someone else with no washing up. You could buy new crockery, making mealtimes more pleasurable by having the opportunity to use your new items. Making your food experience a good one, and something to look forward to, takes the obligation out of eating.

Another great way to enjoy eating is to cook everything you wanted to eat that your ex-spouse didn't. Our lifestyle choices are likely to have been dictated to some degree by our partner, therefore we are now free to make our own choices about the food we eat with no limitations. I started enjoying salads again and onions in things – and I appreciated that, even in the midst of misery and despair.

Lastly, the act of creating something entirely new and different can be quite cathartic, and hopefully delicious, so why not try a new recipe? If it is an unmitigated disaster, don't despair. Order a takeaway! If you have never really cooked, this could be a chance to learn a new skill.

Emotions can have a huge impact on eating, so don't let guilt be the principal one here. Eat when you can and what you can, if you struggle to eat – or hold off when you can, if you are a comfort eater. In the end, eating will become enjoyable again.

Be at home alone

Being home alone, particularly during the evening or at the weekend, can feel dauntingly endless. Different friends said particular days were hardest: for some it was Saturdays, a "family" day, or Sundays – seeing people out and about doing things together and feeling alone. During separation and divorce you are trying to garner the strength to cope with the changes, while simultaneously facing them in many tiny ways every day, expending emotional and physical energy. Well done: it's no mean feat. Feel free to take a break, stay at a friend's house, or have a night away, because living alone can feel like being the last Malteser rattling around in a box.

If you have children, perhaps they offer physical comfort in hugs and snuggling down to watch TV, but if you live alone it can feel incredibly isolated. Research states that a twenty-second hug releases endorphins, so these endorphins can quickly be missed in the absence of a significant other. However, even if other people live with you, the physical space around you can feel magnified in separation. Your spouse is not there. Their presence may have become a burden to you, but you may still miss them. It can feel like a contradiction, but it's easy to forget what was quite so awful before, until they return and it's not as it once was.

Perhaps you have lived on your own before. I had never lived alone, ever, and as such the silence and imposed solitude felt oppressive and stressful. As an extrovert, living alone was extremely difficult for me and I had to gradually build up the time I spent alone at home, learning to enjoy it. I went from coming home only to sleep, to enjoying half an hour of downtime, to eventually spending whole evenings by myself, but it took time to learn to enjoy this rather than endure it. Watching the television, obvious as it sounds, helped to alleviate the silence. We are now readily able to connect with others around the world, which offers us the choice never to be alone. While being alone is important, cathartic, and necessary, it was also extremely hard to bear for extended periods of time. As I mentioned earlier, a friend would regularly Skype me of an evening. The talking itself wasn't overly important; it was more that the companionship which I was so missing was provided by my friend – simply by being at the other end of the screen.

By contrast, introverts may enjoy the opportunity to be alone and to hide away from the world, and this can be as damaging as spending all your time avoiding being alone. If you think you will spend all your time alone, try to arrange one evening a week where you go out. If that feels too much, invite a friend over to spend time with you. Perhaps use a games console to play online and chat with a friend as you play.

However, you can still feel isolated, even when not living alone. Being in a marriage where the other person no longer knows if they want to be there is lonely. In fact, it's incredible just how lonely you can feel with someone who has shut themselves off. They are physically present but emotionally absent. Combine this with the fact that it is your closest, dearest friend who is cutting themselves off from you. Deliberate or not, it is unimaginably isolating.

Living alone can feel like being cut off, but perhaps it is less isolating than we think. By not living with someone who is emotionally absent, we can find ourselves alone but without the extreme loneliness we previously felt. "Alone" is not necessarily the same as "lonely". You *can* be lonely when you're alone. But just because you are alone does not mean you're lonely. As Ellie says in her story at the end of this chapter, there can be plus points. For Carol, it removed the unpredictability she had come to expect, which was much less stressful. It doesn't always mean a purely negative experience, even while it brings its own trials.

Living alone is tiring though: where once there were two, there's now only one to wash up, lock the doors at night, clean, and make the dinner. For a long time, this required an energy I just didn't have. Suddenly being alone can be exhausting. So can being married, but going from two down to one is hard, hard work. There's no one at home to offload to after a hard day, no one to share and halve a problem. That said, there is no one to criticize you and you don't have to try to work out what someone else is feeling. Having a friend you can call or a pet to talk to can alleviate the loneliness and help to avoid isolation, be that desired or not.

Questions to consider

Are you happy living alone or do you find it hard?

What do you enjoy about being by yourself? If your answer is "nothing" – as mine was – what do you enjoy doing when you're alone? Is there a way you can build this into your routine?

Can you think of one positive about living alone?

If you love being alone and in solitude, how might you interact with another person outside of work?

Go out alone

You walk into a room and can almost feel the hush descend; your former partner's absence is a tangible presence. Where are they? Why aren't they here? What's happened? What did you do? What did *they* do? You'd give anything not to be here, but you don't feel you can leave, or avoid the place entirely for the next few years.

Going into church in the wake of separation was a huge challenge for me. We had always attended church together and, naturally, people wondered where he was. Dealing with this was extremely difficult. So much had happened that it was impossible to easily communicate this to other people. It was at church that my closest friends would surround me and protect me from too much social engagement. While there may have been many who could have supported me and shared their own valuable experiences, I only wanted those whom I knew I could trust.

Entering any place the two of you frequented together is likely to give rise to questions. These are often well meaning, but unwelcome. Asking a friend to steer conversations and be an ever-present companion can help to alleviate those awkward moments. Again, our friends are often glad to have something practical and useful and supportive to do for us, so just ask them!

If you're going somewhere that you used to go to as a couple, well done! Don't underestimate the bravery and emotional resilience you're displaying, and if it's too hard to go in – that's completely understandable. When we enter, we are anticipating the potential conversations, questions, and dealing with our own emotional response to the fact they are not there. On different days, you may feel differently, so try not to write off situations after one event. As you go into places you used to go to together, gradually it gets easier. The environment starts to become more "yours" than "ours".

Questions to consider

Are there any places you used to go to together that you would like to return to?

Are there people who might accompany you?

In addition to going places where you both used to go, there is now the absence of a companion to accompany you on general trips out. I like to celebrate my successes – maybe with dinner out. If I've had a miserable or tiring day, I might like to get a coffee and a cake. Essentially most life events lend themselves to some sort of edible experience in my opinion. Except that this is also when I want someone to share it with, but there's not always someone around. This is entirely reasonable. No one's life revolves around me except mine.

But I'm often scared of going alone. "Table for one, please" doesn't trip off my tongue, and what will I do while I'm eating? Read? Just eat? People watch? Will people wonder why I'm alone? How am I meant to read a book while using a knife and fork? Is there anywhere I'll look less conspicuous?

I live in London and have heard it said that it is one of the loneliest cities. It's so easy to feel anonymous in the most enormous crowds. For some the anonymity is relief. Friends who love to go to the cinema alone, or pop to the theatre, or sit and drink coffee by themselves relish the time. In their separation this element didn't phase them at all. This doesn't sit well with me. I want company. It can be silent, but company nonetheless.

My first, enforced, solo-dining experience was a buffet breakfast. Now I love a buffet breakfast – food aplenty, juice, and fresh coffee. What's not to like? I was attending a course and had been put up in a lovely hotel the night before. There was no way I wasn't eating a free and plentiful breakfast, so I went and ate alone. And I didn't know what to do with myself. I observed other lone diners reading the paper, and wished I'd picked one up. I got seconds (obviously), wondering if someone would clear my table thinking no one was sitting there.

It has been a brave and courageous move for me to go, alone, into establishments and sit by myself, not analysing what others might think. I have boldly asked to share a lady's table before, and later someone joined me after she left. If they are anything like me they were far too focused on their tea and cake to care. I can immerse myself in writing, easy enough to do while delicately consuming/ shovelling in cake and sipping/gulping tea. I can observe. I can listen. I overhear singing, good-natured teasing, intriguing conversations.

But being alone can be unnerving. You don't take up a whole table, you wonder what others are thinking, and listening to the animated conversations around you, you begin to wonder whether you should be there at all. But it can also be empowering. You are a whole and complete person by yourself. You are just as entitled to dinner or a trip to the theatre as the next person.

There may be events you go to alone where you will be expected to interact with others. Stepping into a place where you don't know anyone can be intimidating. I don't know who to speak to, and after the welcome where do I fit in? Do I loiter around after the event, or just leave? But going alone is the first step. I often found that if I stood and waited just long enough, people would approach. If I left a space free, someone would take it. Those moments feel like an eternity: the longest, loneliest time. Give yourself a time limit, count to sixty in your head – slowly! It's made me go and talk to people standing alone too.

Meeting new people and having interesting conversations can be bigger than fear. Going to a new place and exploring can be bigger than the pangs of loneliness. Writing to a friend or reading means I'm no longer quite so alone. Entering that room without knowing anyone perhaps allows me to be uniquely myself. The overwhelming sweep of loneliness then magnifies the welcome and friendship extended to me. Being able to go to places by ourselves, even for a few minutes, affirms our character and our bravery. We may not have done this for an incredibly long time; maybe we've never really done this before.

Rather than expect yourself to immediately go alone to everything (unless you are naturally a fan of doing so), make a list of a few places you would be comfortable to go to alone. Perhaps the cinema: sitting in a darkened room where you can go straight in and not worry about whether people are thinking that it's odd you're alone. A coffee shop: take along a book and sit for a while to read. A walk or sit in the park: watch the world go by, appreciate the sights, smells, and sounds around you.

If I had been asked to rate my going-out-alone experiences, coffee shops would have been near the top (providing I had the company of a book), yet dinner alone, or a trip to the theatre would be way down at the bottom. We all react differently to time alone but when it is forced upon you it can be one of the hardest things to endure. Take small steps and don't be afraid to invite others along with you too.

Questions to consider

What intimidates you most about going somewhere alone?

Why does it scare you?

How can you manage this fear and step out alone?
Make a list of a few ways you would be happy to spend time alone.

Go to work

For most people, work probably has the advantage of being one of the spaces where your spouse was not present. Their absence isn't a "thing" because they were never there.

In the numerous times that my marriage, friendship, and dreams seemed irretrievable, I lost count of the number of people who said to me, "Just throw yourself into work." The idea is good: if you are working, you are less likely to be thinking about your personal problems. Work can give your life meaning and stop you from becoming bogged down entirely in your emotions. Essentially, work can help put your feelings on pause.

Whatever your feelings about working at this time, it is good to go if you can. It may also be necessary to have time off, and potentially to be signed off for a period. None of these are the wrong decision. I personally did not find work helpful – my job was stressful and intense in an already intense time – yet the people at work were a huge source of support and an essential part of my everyday survival. I would not have known what to do during the day had I not been at work, so it was valuable to attend and focus, even though often I found it stressful. There were days when I was unable to go in – mentally strained rather than physically exhausted – and took days off, to ensure I maintained my mental health. Mental health is just as important as physical health, and time off work to help you deal with any issues related to this is just as essential as recuperating from a physical illness. If you are unsure of what to do and how to cope with going to work, seek advice from your doctor.

It may be helpful to tell a trusted colleague about your situation. If your manager is approachable, sharing what has happened with them may help them to be sympathetic. There may also be support services you can access through work. Do make sure to check with your HR manager.

Yet be careful of using work to give your life all its meaning. While you may have felt marriage was your security and now hold on to work, among other things, I believe that ultimately the only thing that can give your life the deep meaning it needs is God. Work may change: God is constant. People may change: God is constant. Our challenge in embracing work is to simultaneously hold it loosely in our grasp, rather than considering it the one certainty in a world of shifting sands. Even if you do not believe in God, your work will not fill a gap in your identity left by a broken relationship. That said, work may be a helpful constant at this time – something steady and known. But it will evolve eventually, so if we pin our identity to work instead of our relationship we are liable to be hurt once again.

It may be that your ex *is* present at work. If this is the case, you might need to draw particular boundaries around conduct and conversation in order to work effectively together. For example, it would be wise to only discuss work matters when at work and refuse to speak about your personal relationship. Remember that your colleagues may also be your ex's colleagues. Telling your ex who you have spoken to at work about your relationship breakdown can be difficult, but it also shows them that you are treating them with respect.

Questions to consider

Is there a colleague or colleagues you can speak to?

Are you using your work as a core part of your identity?

What makes you passionate about what you do? Use this passion to help spur you on at work.

Do you need to seek support at work or take time off? Remember that mental health is as important as physical health.

Ellie's story

Divorce is something I never thought I would have to face. Perhaps naively, I had assumed it happened to people who made bad decisions about the person they married, or those who weren't prepared to work at a relationship. I found out the hard way that it can happen to anyone.

My ex-husband and I used to have a great relationship. We had lots of fun, close family and friends, and busy social lives, and were part of a church community. I think this is why it was such a massive shock when everything suddenly fell apart. It felt like my whole world had turned upside down.

After a few weeks of not seeming himself, I pushed my ex-husband to tell me why. Little did I know what was to ensue. He told me he was in love with another woman and wasn't sure if he still wanted the life we had built together. It was several months later that he finally admitted he had been having an affair.

I can't describe the emotional pain I went through. It felt so unfair the way it had come seemingly out of the blue, and that I didn't have a choice in it, even though the consequences would affect every aspect of my life for ever. I fought to make the relationship work, which meant living in limbo for more than a year and a half, but sadly after six years of marriage (nine years together in total) he chose divorce.

To begin with I focused on survival, just getting through one day at a time because I couldn't bear to think any further ahead. However, several years on I can look back and see that I have thrived. I have learned to be grateful for all the people and things I have. I have learned to be vulnerable and honest with people, and have developed amazingly deep friendships as a result. My faith has grown because I have found that I can trust God in any circumstance. I have taken opportunities to pursue different dreams, including living in Africa, moving to London, and changing careers. My life now looks very different compared with before, and in many ways I feel like a different person. I am more aware of my weaknesses but am also stronger and more courageous.

I have chosen to share my story because I don't want separation and divorce to be something that people can't talk about, especially in church; the elephant in the room, as it were! I was greatly encouraged by talking to others who had endured similar situations, and I hope our stories will provide some comfort and hope.

Chapter Three

Talking about Divorce and Separation

How did you respond to the probing question, "How are you?"

Rowena: Probably by deflection. The obvious answer is, "I'm doing terribly", but do people really want to hear that, unless they are a really close friend? Other people just didn't know what to say and that gets awkward.

Decobe: I've always been a very open person. Some have voiced that I am a bit too open at times about myself. But that's the way I am. So when asked, "How are you?" the questioner usually always got the full truth and I answered completely and honestly. Besides which, the look on my face probably said it all. This may have even shocked them. Perhaps that's why a lot of so-called friends disappeared! Perhaps they wanted to hear something else, something more positive or something they could deal with. Some really good friends, however, dug in deep and rode out the storm with me, and remain some of my closest friends today.

Carol: I would normally just say, "I'm fine" unless I obviously wasn't… I'm not much good at hiding how I feel. If it were a good friend I'd be really honest. If it were an acquaintance I would just say, "It's a tough day, but I'm fine". Most people knew so didn't need to really ask. At work it was much easier to just say the normal platitudes to be polite.

Ellie: This changed a lot through the whole ordeal. With my close friends and family I was brutally honest about the rollercoaster of emotions right from the start. They were incredibly sympathetic and spent many hours listening. But with most friends, family, and colleagues I was quick to divert the conversation away from what was going on and talk about anything else. Over time, as I realized our marriage had broken down so much it might not recover, I opened up a lot to anyone I trusted, or even if I didn't know them particularly well, if I sensed I could trust them. I've heard it said that we impress people with our strengths but connect with them through our weaknesses and I found that was the case.

May: When asked how I was, it depended on whether it was a trusted close friend or not as to whether I would tell the truth. I could say "coping" or talk about things I enjoyed doing. Or if I trusted them, I could say I was having some counselling which was helpful.

Explaining your partner's absence

At some point you will have to leave the house and interact with others because, much as you might want to, spending the next few years under a duvet is not a practical choice. While being alone and perhaps surviving life in the environs you once shared can be monumentally difficult, leaving the house and needing to interact with others holds its own challenges. If people know you well, they may notice you're not OK. The notable absence of your spouse may result in well-meaning questions that you find incredibly hard to answer. Yet being outside the home may also be a huge relief: a welcome respite from the need to analyse or think through emotions and actions. So when are the times we may encounter others and need to tell them about our situation? Work and church are two of the biggest situations in which I found myself at a vulnerable point, as well as in social situations where we had joint friends. Bumping into someone in the supermarket only to be asked the question, "So, how's X?" can be enough to make you want to crumple to the floor and cry. Being able to manage these moments and having a strategy to cope there and then before retreating to a safe space means that we don't need to dread them in quite the same way.

To begin with, it is important to consider how we feel when we even think of speaking about our relationship breakdown. Try to imagine telling someone, maybe a close friend, or perhaps an acquaintance. Which words would you use to describe what has happened? How difficult is it to begin? Or is it too hard to imagine? If it is too much, or you simply don't know what to say, that's entirely normal. Describing divorce and separation isn't easy. There is so much to explain.

Finding the words

Explaining to people what has happened may be a necessity for one reason or another: you may need their support, or just want to let them know. Choosing the words with which to convey this message can be hard. Each word you choose is loaded with meaning – "we're separated", "our marriage has broken down", "it's failed, ended, over". There are so few positive words to describe separation and divorce. Personally, I found there were two words that made my skin crawl, my stomach lurch, and helped tear my heart and mind in two: failure and separation.

My marriage had failed. We had failed. I had failed. Failed to be a good enough wife, a strong enough couple. Failed to do whatever was necessary to make our marriage survive. Of the many words about the end of a marriage, this smarted the most. The connotations of failure are blame, guilt, and an absolute sense of somehow being "not enough". It is interesting that people who are divorced don't often talk about a "failed" marriage. They will talk about their marriage ending or breaking down, or their "first" marriage – regardless of whether they've married again or not! "Failed" assumes you did not meet the expectation – married unto death; and in that sense "failed" is true. It did not meet the golden standard for marriage.

But whose marriage is perfect? I defy any of us to feel that marriage never disappoints, or that our spouse hasn't or didn't at one time let us down. Truthfully, we will all have neglected our other half, even if unintentionally.

Despite what anyone may say about your marriage, you are not a failure. Divorced, happily married, single: you are not a failure. You are human. The Bible tells us that we all fall short of the glory of God. I fall short daily (Romans 3:23). I fell short in my marriage. If I get married again, I imagine that despite my very best efforts, I will fall short once more.

Did my marriage fail? I guess it did. But I can choose the words I want to use about my situation. For a long time, explaining that we were separated felt like knocking a further nail in the coffin. Eventually, I began to say that we were living separately, instead of being "separated". Now it doesn't faze me to explain what happened, but it has taken considerable time to get to this point.

Certain words and phrases carry a particular weight. Saying, "he/she decided to leave" may feel less raw than "he/she left me". Describing actions as choices or decisions may help you to come to terms with the way in which you or your ex-spouse behaved. There is no ideal way to describe what has happened, but simply what feels comfortable to you. I have heard people describe their marriage as "completed", rather than failed. Your marriage may have produced children, but it will almost certainly have produced moments of happiness. It is up to you how to describe your marriage. My marriage may have failed, but I did not. I am more than the sum total of one life event, as are you.

Questions to consider

Which words upset you most when describing your relationship? What is it about these words that you find challenging?

Which words help you to honestly explain what has happened?

Practise telling a close friend what has happened to decide on the best wording for you. Telling people can be freeing, but don't feel obliged to disclose anything you don't want to.

Responding to invasive questions

While some avoid subjects they know might be sensitive, or don't want to pry, it seems others have no qualms questioning you about your life: "Are you going to have children?"; "When are you going to pop the question?" Major life decisions seem to give some people permission to say pretty much anything. During separation and divorce such invasive questions can become increasingly difficult to answer. There is such intense personal pain and confusion that you don't want to share it with everyone and you may feel quite angry at being asked. You may not fully understand the situation you've been placed in; maybe it's all up in the air and can't be described in a succinct manner. Perhaps you've made a decision to leave and that means you are open to unwanted and unwelcome scrutiny from those who don't really know you or your marriage. You may not want to share the whys and wherefores of your marital difficulties. And frankly – that's OK!

It can be hard to engage in conversation when you just want to yell at everyone to "leave me alone". To try and counter this, I would prepare answers in advance. Whenever I was asked how my ex was, I was partially honest and told people he wasn't well, as I believed he was depressed. I didn't elaborate on where he was living or on any aspect of our relationship to start with. Over time I became more honest and said I thought he was OK, or eventually, when I felt able to acknowledge that we no longer lived together, that I didn't know how he was.

How will you respond to the question, "So, where's your husband/wife/partner?"

I hate to be rude and feel out of sorts with someone, but sometimes responding, "Thank you for your concern, but I really don't want to/can't talk about that at the moment" to this question was a necessary conversation stopper. My gentleness or bluntness was dictated by the repetition or intrusiveness of the question. On one occasion I was grilled with several questions, one after another, culminating with, "Did you have an affair? Did he have an affair?" I was shocked they'd had the gall to ask it and refused to answer any of their questions with a very straightforward, "I'm not going to answer that." After that, I avoided all situations in which I might be questioned by them in the future, which wasn't easy due to our close proximity in daily life. It sounds extreme perhaps, but it did stop me from feeling any obligation to respond and react.

I simply didn't want to talk about it. I garnered the courage to be blunt, hoped people would understand – and if they didn't, then I probably didn't want to share my experiences with them anyway. Those closest to me knew I could not cope with certain questions and would stay close to me when we were out together. They could interrupt, redirect the conversation or take over completely if they saw me floundering. People are also less likely to ask you very probing personal questions in a group scenario; it's simply not appropriate. Sometimes people asked me how I was and I would try to quickly redirect the conversation. Usually, I would speak about work, which as a teacher provided endless scope for story (or in my case complaint), or about my family as at that time my brother was about to get married. It is highly likely these were not the answers they were seeking, but it was a valid way to field difficult questions.

How did you respond to ,"How's your other half?"

Decobe: This wasn't generally a problem for me, as nearly everybody I met day-to-day knew of the situation and refrained from asking me about it. This may have been to prevent themselves from being hurt by the answer, or to prevent causing me more pain. This isn't to say that the situation wasn't discussed, but usually only if I prompted the conversation. If the question was asked by someone who wasn't aware of the situation, then I wasn't very complimentary about my other half or her new partner. In fact, I probably came over as a rather bitter and twisted person at times. Most of the time, I wasn't really sure where she was or what she was doing; just that she had gone to live with another man and that we were going to get a divorce. Occasionally, I heard things from my daughter about what her mum was doing, but tried not to let the pain show on my face. I wanted to protect my daughter from the pain I was going through.

Rowena: While I was at my parents' house, this wasn't really a problem. When I got back to Germany, it was a bit different. He was away again though – that was pretty normal, him being in the army – and people didn't really ask that much.

Carol: I would just say whatever rolled off my tongue at the time, depending on who was asking and how I was feeling. Generally, I would just say, "I don't really know as we're not together now." Most people knew the situation so weren't surprised. It was more difficult when business clients asked, so I would just say, "He's fine".

Ellie: For quite a while I only told close friends about what was going on because I wanted to protect him and our marriage. To other people I would say something truthful and non-descript, like, he was at his parents, then swiftly move the conversation on. I didn't feel obliged to share my darkest feelings with just anyone who asked. However, once we'd been separated for several months and it was clear there would be no quick fix, I tended to be blunt and say we were separated. I didn't want it to be the elephant in the room! I think a lot of people could tell something was going on but didn't dare ask me – some asked my sister or friends instead. I had fab friends who were like wingmen for me, ready to deflect conversations and make sure I was OK.

May: My ex had an accident and has scarring to the frontal brain lobe. This caused brain damage and a change of personality. People at church asked me how he was when they saw me alone. Many thought he had been completely healed, as the head injury was a hidden one. This was frustrating – people even asked me if he wasn't "quite all there". I would say that my ex was still giving money away and was addicted to meeting women in chat rooms on the internet. He had a girlfriend. There were some people with whom I gave up socializing, and I sought out new friends instead.

Eventually, it becomes easier to talk about aspects of your marriage, separation, and divorce. But there's never an obligation to share with anyone. It's fine to refuse to answer a question. It is your life, your business, and it's up to you who you talk to.

Questions to consider

What information are you willing to share? What do you want to keep private?

What are you concerned about being asked? Make a list of questions. Draft answers to these and practise them on an encouraging and supportive friend.

What other conversational topics would you feel happy discussing? Try to have one of these at the forefront of your mind to move the conversation on to, even if it feels like an unnatural shift – they should get the hint!

Pronouns

I? We? Me? Us? A lesser-discussed part of divorce is the confusing world of the pronoun. It sounds like a stupid problem in a way, but in the initial stages of separation, "us" has ended and now there is only "me". Getting used to being singular rather than plural is an immense shift in thinking – uttering the pronoun merely enhances the loneliness. Your part in a partnership is no more. It's a gradual transition from being one of two to a singleton. After a while it comes more naturally: you don't have to force yourself to remember. You use "I" to speak about yourself, and don't trip over the pronoun.

But then comes the second problem of pronouns. Once the singular pronoun can be uttered without wanting to burst into tears, what about the past? There used to be "us" but it doesn't feel appropriate to say so any more. With close friends it's irrelevant and you can refer to the two of you together, but in talking to others it can be a semantic minefield. We went to lots of places, we shared lots of experiences, we quite clearly had a wedding, but sometimes it was easier to pretend it was just "me" who did those things alone, and to keep quiet when there was any wedding talk.

It can feel like you have to hide part of your life. Why would you want to talk about your wedding and the emotions of the day when it has ended so badly? Only a few years after separation, did I become comfortable with referring to us both if context demanded it. It's true – it happened, and that's just part of my story. Saying, "my ex and I" leaves the marital context vague while being clear we're no longer attached to one another. Sometimes, I still, years on, keep it simple and erase whole swathes of my past so that it just contains me. One day they might know, and if not, does it matter? We are still ourselves, creating new memories, embracing new experiences, and continuing to confuse people with our grammatical inaccuracies.

Questions to consider

Do you feel comfortable talking about your ex-spouse and explaining the situation if asked?

Are there friends with whom you can discuss events involving your ex-spouse?

Would being vague or speaking in the singular be more straightforward initially?

Chapter Four

Coping with the Day-to-day

Household chores

Chances are, before you split up, household tasks were somehow apportioned between you. Now, the responsibility lies entirely with you. That prospect, on top of emotional exhaustion, is harrowing. I found that keeping things together was a struggle I regularly lost. Washing basket: overflowing. Washing up: piled high. If I'm honest, this hasn't changed a whole lot but that's now mainly because I don't make time to do these things. Washing up, washing, ironing, tidying, vacuuming, dusting: the list of things to do to keep a home running felt endless. Things like emptying the bin, checking the oil in the car, and changing a lightbulb weren't even on my radar, yet now they needed to be. Literally *every* task fell to me. But before the sheer abundance of things to do overwhelms you, break them down.

What were the most practical solutions you found to coping with day-to-day life?

Carol: Work! And actually meeting friends again. I hadn't really realized but during my marriage I had gradually reduced contact with them all because it was easier not to see them than to be constantly moaning about him and then being told to leave him. I felt most of them didn't really get my commitment to the vows I'd made.

Decobe: Keeping my "mind" busy helped considerably. As I read Simon Guillebaud's daily readings from *Choose Life*, it reminds me that somewhere I must have felt an element of hope among all the despair.

May: To help deal with the changes resulting from his head injury I joined a carers' group and we had joint CBT (Cognitive Behavioural Therapy) sessions for a while, as well as separate individual sessions. I made sure I met up with a good friend with whom I discussed things and we prayed together regularly. I took up sailing again and also occasionally played badminton – a welcome break from doing reams of paperwork and accounts for the divorce.

Ellie: Initially, it was a challenge not to think too far ahead and to worry about the possible consequences of his decision. Should I change my name? Where would I live? What would I do? One of the most helpful bits of advice I was given was to only focus on getting through that particular day and not think further ahead.

Rowena: Keeping busy and seeing good friends.

Within some marriage preparation courses – one of which you may have taken part in – there is an activity in which each person attributes a percentage of responsibility for household tasks between their mother and father. The purpose of the activity is to establish perceived expectations in marriage and how this may then impact the future of your marriage. Now the responsibility has entirely fallen at your door. By working out what responsibilities your spouse held, you will be able to consider how to manage these effectively yourself, even under this extreme pressure.

While this is not an exhaustive list, it may begin to help to think through areas of daily life where regular upkeep is necessary:

- *laundry: washing, ironing, dry-cleaning*
- *food: shopping, cooking, washing up*
- *cleaning: tidying, mopping, vacuuming, dusting*
- *bills: water, electricity, gas, phone, mortgage/rent*
- *insurance: house, contents, car*
- *car care: services, annual safety checks, upkeep*
- *gardening*

Make your own list of tasks carried out around the home – it doesn't need to be exhaustive as you can add to it as things crop up. This list may feel extremely daunting, but it does not all need to be managed now. Your aim in making the list is to identify what might need doing, not to do all those things right away.

Questions to consider

What were you and your partner's main household tasks?

What was your spouse responsible for in the home? Make a list of things they took charge of.

Time management

If financially possible, consider paying for people to assist you in some of these chores. This isn't a cop-out. There were two of you; now you're simply paying someone to fill in that gap. It can be hard to decide whether the time or the money is worth more, and that trade-off may change later, but right now there is an immediate need for help, and it's perfectly acceptable to pay for it, if you can afford to do so. If you are time or energy poor, this is a great strategy.

If it isn't possible financially to get help, consider allocating jobs to particular days or times of the day so that they don't hang over you. Having a particular day on which to do laundry meant I knew how long I would need to last with my clean clothes and favourite outfits; while having a cut-off date for the vacuuming helped me not to feel I was living in a grubby and uncomfortable place. Vacuuming was (and still is) my least favourite chore, so there was even some sense of satisfaction in accomplishing it. A pitfall of this philosophy is our ability to guilt trip ourselves if we don't achieve this. However, this structure is there to help you, not to condemn you. By missing a day it is unlikely anyone will be seriously hurt by waiting longer for a particular outfit or by a lack of vacuuming. It just means you might need to do two chores on a particular day instead of one.

Alternatively, if you know of people with particular passions, ask them for help. I wish I had been one of those people for whom cleaning is a stress reliever. I do love a clean and tidy space, but my inclination to keep it so wanes with every stressor. I feel I would have found life easier if even a tiny fibre of my being had enjoyed chores of any description. But knowing my best friend found great joy in bringing order to chaos was very helpful. I could ask for genuine, practical help that made an untold difference to my week. To be able to don rubber gloves and leave a gleaming kitchen was a pleasure to her, and a complete gift to me. Particularly with my reluctance to clean, having help with daily chores and the occasional spring or winter -clean made the whole experience much more bearable, even if others simply sat there and chatted to me while I cleaned. Knowing which friends enjoyed being able to help practically, meant I felt able to ask them if they could be around. It is often much easier to put someone else's chaos into order than your own, and somehow more enjoyable too.

It is also helpful to remember friends who have particular skills. When I arrived home to a very stressed neighbour who had water coming through her ceiling, ostensibly from my flat, I called particular people – those who I knew to be good at DIY, who might know where to begin – when all I wanted to do (and did do) was sit on the floor and have a good cry. They took over the investigations, and while I still had to deal with neighbourly communication, the management agency, and the financial implications, the immediate assistance and knowledgeable support was invaluable. Don't be afraid to ask people who are good at these things. They will say no if they're not able to help, yet they will likely be glad to offer assistance.

Insurance and bills

To help you keep track of bills, make a note of the date on which each one is due to be paid on a calendar. You could also set up a reminder on your phone. Although the bills which have been set up with direct debit get paid automatically, it's worth checking your bank statement to keep a track of payments. You can also allocate a day to deal with any upcoming payments, rather than having the stress of leaving things to the last moment.

If you have financially savvy friends, you can always enlist their help to make sure you're getting the best price for the utilities and services you use. But don't feel under pressure to change every deal or supplier. There may be cheaper options, but if that is not your primary consideration, there is also great value in knowing what you'll be paying.

It is also necessary to consider which name each bill is paid in. Should your ex-spouse continue to pay the bills and be happy to engage in that area of support, there might be no need to change them. If, however, a bill is in your ex-spouse's name alone, it does become more challenging once you wish to speak to someone about it. Changing the bill to incorporate your name too may be a good solution, or you may wish to leave it as a joint payment in order that they are kept accountable for the financial side too. Should you wish to have a payment in your name only, you could frame it to your ex-spouse that you are seeking to free them from a burden. Gaining ownership over your own finances can be remarkably liberating and can help you to move on.

If there are debts in their or your name, seek financial advice about changing names or accounts, as it may be preferable to leave these as they are until any financial divorce negotiations are finalized. Free appointments with financial advisors can be made at your bank, or through organizations such as CAP (Christians Against Poverty),[6] where you do not need to be of the faith to seek support.

Questions to consider

What bills do you have to pay?

When do they need to be paid/renewed?

Are they in your name? Do you need to contact the company to change them from/into your name?

---

6   https://capuk.org/

Chapter Five

Taking Time Out

If life were a movie

When my marriage began to break down, one of the thoughts I regularly had was that if only life were a movie, two years would be done in two hours. In two hours you can go through all the emotions of grief and emerge, if not yet triumphant, then at least a little bit hopeful. Imagine a movie such as *P.S. I Love You* or *Taken*: polar opposites as movies, but with one thing in common – the trauma is done in two hours. We get very used to watching entire weeks of someone's life, or even years, pass by in moments, and it makes it hard to realize that our own do not.

While living through two years of separation and divorce proceedings had felt an eternity each day, by the time it was over I was, quite literally, in a completely different place – on holiday with my oldest childhood friend, a new job on the horizon. Almost unbelievably, I was actually happy, while still in the process of mourning my marriage. If I could have foreseen this at the beginning of my marriage breakdown, maybe it would have given me hope. But equally, there are many things I would not have learned, experienced, or achieved along the way. These weren't all good experiences or positive times, but they've certainly created who I am now.

I have no idea how far along your experience of separation or divorce you are but try and think back two years. Chances are, things were somewhat different. Maybe you look back and think how happy you were. Maybe you look back and see a couple suffering in a marriage that wasn't working. But if you compare then to now, it is likely that there will be major differences. Now think how much can change in two years. That is something to hold on to.

Questions to consider

What did life look like two years ago? (It may be necessary to grieve this change as you consider it.)

How might your life look different in two years' time? Add in any unfulfilled dreams you might like to achieve, however adventurous or impossible they may seem right now.

The difficulty of looking towards the future is that we're still required to live in the day-to-day. Whether you knew your marriage was having difficulties or the announcement was a bolt from the blue, there are many decisions to be made – some of which we have already considered. Sometimes, though, we need to simply stop, and the following section explores our time and how to use it wisely when both it, and we, are under pressure.

Life on hold

Solomon, a biblical king known for his wisdom, wrote that "hope deferred makes the heart sick".[7] There are moments that may make us want to put life on hold. Acknowledging that you need time out to process your emotions can be the first step toward recovery.

As a child in the early nineties I watched a TV show called *Bernard's Watch*. Bernard's watch was special: with it he could stop time, rewind, and change the course of events before life continued

---

7   Proverbs 13:12, ESV.

– with no one realizing, of course. Everyone who saw it wanted it. It was the dream. One episode I really remember (mild peril alert) is when Bernard's friend's rabbit was about to be run over having escaped its hutch, and Bernard stopped time, heroically saved the rabbit, and averted disaster. Why this particular episode ingrained itself in my mind I have no idea as I'm not overly fond of rabbits; I did, however, want a watch like Bernard's – who wouldn't?

We encounter this "stop the world feeling" fairly regularly. There is little worse than feeling you can do nothing to resolve a situation that it is entirely out of your hands and that you are dependent on other people in order to have the problem solved. Humans like to fix things. We like to sort things out, to resolve situations. When that ability is taken away from us, we want the world to stop; we want to be able to work it out, to know, and to understand. We want to put life on pause like Bernard did until we've figured it out.

I would have given everything to be able to stop time, rewind, and change the course of events surrounding my marriage breakdown. Yet I could not. I was required to continue living in a world that did not know the cataclysmic change and destruction that had occurred within my life and within me.

As the initial impact of marital breakdown hits, we want the world to pause while we catch up and try to make sense of what has happened. It's important to stay aware of the emotions associated with separation and divorce and the depth of your feelings. We can all feel, especially at these times, that we can't keep going, but if you feel you may be depressed or if you have suicidal thoughts you also need to seek professional help.

Some of the best "life on pause" advice I received came from my friend Rob. "Buy yourself a box set," he said. "One with lots of episodes that you haven't seen before and then when it's all too much, watch one, and because you haven't seen it before, you have to concentrate." Essentially: escape. I'm not a natural back-to-back episode watcher –

although I finally discovered *The West Wing* about fifteen years after everyone else – but usually I would rather be doing something other than watching TV. That said, I wish I'd taken his advice sooner. When I did eventually invest (in *Sherlock*), it was like putting the world on pause. The series I'd chosen required intense concentration purely to keep up, and for an hour I could just forget my life. Or indeed, for a few hours as I watched more than one series back to back. I couldn't consider my own problems if I wanted to keep up with the programme – there simply wasn't the headspace. I also found it incredibly helpful that there was no particular romance or love story. I was surprised it worked. It was so different from anything I might have usually chosen to do (such as read or socialize), yet the opportunity to switch off my mind from my own problems for an hour was invaluable.

Perhaps your pause button is not something you would have expected, so be open to suggestions. Somehow, though, putting life on pause, in whatever way works for the individual, realigns us with who we are. For that hour-long episode, I was just the me who likes logic and puzzle-solving and who wanted to solve the mystery.

What distractions would help you stop and put life "on pause"?

As helpful as it can be to put aside emotions and thoughts, we need to remember to come back to them in order to effectively process them, or they can return, often intrusively and with detrimental effect. Talking to friends may help – being able to rant and rave about the situation in a safe and loving environment can be beneficial. You may find it helpful to go for a run or a walk; a close friend and I describe it as "pounding the pavements". Being on your own can actually help you to process emotions. You could try writing things down, though I would avoid sending a steaming email of emotion to your ex. Healthy management of feelings allows them to come to the fore and be acknowledged, so it's worth considering when and where you feel safe. Not acknowledging sadness and negative emotions and then, as a consequence, letting them overwhelm your soul does not allow you the space to grieve what you've lost.

You have been hurt. Feeling angry, aggrieved, devastated, and lost are all natural ways to feel. Giving yourself time to be these things is being kind to yourself. We need to allow time for our wounds to heal. It can be easy to assume that we ought to be OK or to put emotions to one side and ignore them while they heal. But if we did this with a burn, the resulting scar would be worse. Ensuring we have ways to tend these emotional wounds will help the scars to heal over as life goes on.

How did you put life "on pause"?

Decobe: During the earlier years after the divorce, I was kept very busy with my job, and the workload just kept on increasing, which took my mind off things during the working day. I also did as much overtime as I could physically manage, just to eke out the hours. During evenings and weekends I watched a lot of television or watched and listened to my increasing collection of DVDs and CDs. Some of my CDs, however, being mostly classical music, rather dragged me down into further depths of misery. As a Christian I also threw myself into spending more time with God and started to really enjoy my relationship with Him. He filled the void in my heart. I even had thoughts of giving my whole life over to Him by entering a monastery and becoming a monk. These thoughts were quite appealing but I soon realized that while it seemed a good idea, it was just a means of escaping from reality and it wasn't the answer. My children, especially my quadriplegic son, had a strong call on me and I couldn't take myself out of their lives. I had a daughter who was soon to be married and there were things for me to help sort out for that event to take place.

Rowena: I played hours of electronic chess. My dad had one of those electronic boards where you could play against the computer. It got to the stage where I won – all the time!

Carol: I had a business to run which took up most of my time. With driving long distances and the stress of that I was pretty tired most of the time so I'd get in, eat, watch some TV, and generally fall asleep on the sofa. I did have lodgers from time to time, and at the weekends I got involved in church. I had good friends who took me under their wing.

Ellie: Work was a massive distraction for me because teaching is always so full on. It all happened when I was supposed to be going into a new school to show them how to improve their maths teaching – it was that or sit at home crying. Somehow I managed it, and it actually went well. Another welcome distraction was decorating my flat. This was much later on, once it transpired that I was going to be on my own either for a while or permanently. I'm no DIY expert but it was nice to look out for things to treat myself to and to make my own decisions. Having friends come over to help out made that bit a positive part of the whole ghastly experience.

May: To help deal with stressful situations I often went away at weekends or sometimes stayed with friends midweek. One summer I did some house-sitting as things were so unbearable.

Questions to consider

Where is your safe space? Where can you give free rein to your emotions without fear of offending or being judged?

How often are you able to be in your safe space?

Are you an external processor? If so, is there a friend or professional who could help you to work through some emotions?

Are there any places where you feel under particular pressure yet do not feel safe to share your emotion?

Consider how you will best cope at the moment and try not to think too far ahead. Things will look different later on. Focus on the now.

Where am I investing my time?

It may be that having the opportunity to focus on something else other than personal circumstance is helpful. Whether we are investing in supporting someone else, additional work, or volunteering, we should be mindful of whether we are in a place to give out. While we don't have to think and reflect on our situation all the time, it is necessary to have thinking space too. In the same way that grief may mean the mind and body need time out to think, consider whether you would be best served by a sabbatical – a period of time off, if your employer offers this.

Now if you're anything like me, the fear may be that you will be letting people down, especially if there is no one to step into your place. When you step back, others may or may not step in to fill the void, but this is not your responsibility. There is only one you. Only you can preserve yourself and ensure that you are taking enough time for yourself. It isn't selfish to step back – sometimes it's necessary. At times you have been, and will be, able to give more of your time and energy to others. At other times, you need to say no to things that have been part of your life and focus on giving your energy to the essential things. The guilt that accompanies this is because we care about our responsibilities and take them seriously. But if we are spending our working hours with people who care about us and value us, they will understand we have to care for ourselves too.

It might be that the reverse is true. Volunteering or supporting another person may give your life the energy and purpose that you feel has been lacking. As with becoming heavily invested in work, it's good to consider whether your identity is becoming tied up in these things to compensate for your marriage, or whether they are a just a healthy part of yourself. Finding a new venture in which to invest time may be a life-saving part of your post-separation life. I found devoting time to writing and blogging hugely helpful as I knew it helped others, and it helped me to rediscover writing, which I'd long loved, but which I'd forgotten about. Volunteering or giving our time to a particular venture may help us learn who we are again.

There isn't a "right" way to do things. Indeed, at different times different things may be right for you, and only you can fully determine which they are. That said, seek the advice of close friends too if you're having trouble deciding. It is not a bad thing to take time for yourself: you are allowed to put you first.

Questions to consider

Are the activities you're investing time in giving you time to reflect too?

Are they exhausting you or energizing you?

May's story

I was married for eight years altogether, and for about two years happily! My ex-husband had a cycling accident only eight months after we married, causing a severe brain injury. He suffered trauma to the head and was a "three", or "totally unresponsive", on the Glasgow Coma Scale. After a few days he briefly opened his eyes and could sometimes press your hand with his when you held it.

Amazingly, he recovered enough to be able to walk again, and his fatigue decreased. However, his personality changed a great deal, and due to the trauma he lost many memories from eight months prior to the accident, and some after the accident. So he didn't remember our wedding and thought I was his girlfriend.

I looked after him and had to take time off work to do that, but I set up some care arrangements so that I could go back to work, part time initially. After about two years he was deemed recovered enough to manage his own finances by a neurologist. Six months after this he started giving large sums of money away to women he had met on the internet. I found a pile of Moneygram receipts in a drawer while I was cleaning and tidying, and went into shock. I called in at my local church for some help to deal with the situation.

He denied everything. I called the neurologist and sent evidence so that financial capacity could be taken away from him. He did stop giving away money for a bit, but then once he had a cash-in-hand job he started again, like an addict. Eventually, he wanted to marry some of the girls he had met on the internet and asked me for a divorce.

The divorce took a long time, since the insurance claim for his head injury had to be resolved first. They had to wait for maximum recovery, and after about five years there was enough information for us to be able to divorce. My solicitor advised me to stay in the house. However, due to his frequent mood changes and addictions I found it difficult to live with him. When things were really unbearable I house-sat for friends and looked after their cats while they were away. I also started renting a room a couple of nights a week, but kept my address as the marital home.

We tried to stay on speaking terms, but used email and text for important things so I had a record of them and so that emotions would not get in the way. Since the divorce we have tried to stay amicable and occasionally meet up. For me it is important to meet new friends as well as to keep in touch with a few previous ones, and to start doing new things.

PART TWO

Moving Forward

Chapter Six

Separating Lives

Separation

Choosing to separate can be a very difficult decision. Reconciliation may feel more likely if you stay living together, experiencing each other's daily lives, and having incidental conversations as well as deep, meaningful talks. There may not be a choice about separating: perhaps you or your spouse have left the marital home and do not intend to return. Perhaps, having left, you or your partner are refusing to live together again. If you are still living together, the decision to separate is an extremely difficult one; it can feel like a signal to the outside world that "this is over". Physical separation does not mean that conversation, support, and working at restoring your marriage has to stop. Equally, living together does not mean these things automatically happen. Friends of mine separated for almost a year, working through personal and marital issues, before living together once more: this was twelve years of marriage and two children ago.

Separation does not simply mean that you are physically apart. It can mean detaching your life from the life of your spouse through non-communication, refusal to engage in any proactive work around the marriage, or avoiding physical intimacy, as well as physically moving out. In this section of the book, we explore how we can separate as amicably and as fairly as possible, and how to begin to re-imagine your space and belongings in the marital home or in a new location.

It may be that one of you feels entitled to remain in the marital home. If there are actions on one side that have led to the collapse of the marriage, it may be most appropriate for that spouse to move out. It may be that the location of your home is necessary for one spouse in their occupation or physical needs. Perhaps one spouse's family is closer and offers accommodation. You may decide that for financial, marital, or familial reasons, it is better for you to both live in the house together. There are, again, no right or wrong answers to this – only what works well and best for you as a couple and as a family.

Who moved out of the marital home?

Carol: Tricky one to answer! I suppose I did but he then manipulated the situation so I let him move back in with me in my new house. However, he slept in the spare room from then on. I eventually got rid of him when I sold the house.

Decobe: She did initially, but a few months later she asked if she and her new partner could move back in as she was buying me out of the home anyway. I moved into a nearby house belonging to some friends and undertook some decorating for them as a way of recompense.

May: Once almost divorced with a decree absolute I moved out of the marital home. In fact, I moved out the day before the final hearing in court since, prior to the previous one, ridiculous stories had been made up about me and I didn't want this to happen again.

Deciding to separate

Deciding to separate can feel like an admission that the marriage is not working or that you've given up. Other people's perceptions and interpretations are not what is important though. As a married couple only you can know the complexities of the relationship and what will be the best and healthiest way for your marriage to proceed.

There are (you may be disappointed to learn) no rules to separation. If you separate, it does not mean you can't reunite. That said, it does not mean you will. Living together may be preferable, yet equally you may need space from one another to work through personal and marital problems. It is important for both of you to clarify why and how any separation will occur. Perhaps it would be more helpful for each of you to seek support from others so that the emotional burden on both of you is eased. Perhaps, until you are fully confident of your commitment to one another, you have decided to focus on your emotional relationship rather than the physical. If you choose something like this, make time to be honest with one another about how you are each coping.

Throughout our separation, we lived together and separately. In the four months after our marriage broke down, I lived with friends for several weeks. At that point I gained physical and emotional strength from their support and, after a time, decided to move back into my own home. My spouse was reluctant for this to happen, yet did not move out, and so we then lived together for two months. At the time I did not describe this as a separation: after all, we lived together! But in many senses, separation had happened. We were speaking, but not really communicating. We were seeking our major emotional support from sources other than, and mostly excluding, each other. We were functioning within the same spaces, but mostly not at the same times. We were sleeping in separate bedrooms. When I asked him either to move out or to re-engage in trying to work things through, it was because I could no longer countenance this way of living separately yet together.

If you are deciding whether to separate, it is valuable to consider all the different elements of your life together to establish the way in which you have grown apart.

Questions to consider

Consider the following areas of your life: day-to-day communication, household tasks, physical intimacy, emotional support. What are your levels of engagement with one another?

If you have stayed living together, why is that? Is it for mutual convenience, or through a commitment to one another?

Are you safer living apart? Do not stay in a situation in which you are in danger.

Are your living arrangements impacting on your ability to work positively towards reconciling?

If appropriate, what steps are you each taking towards reconciliation?

Will you set up regular conversations to consider the direction your marriage is moving in?

Living together while separated

There is no ideal way to separate or divorce but living together while you are separated poses its own particular challenges.

As a married couple there is a sharing of responsibilities. Taking out the bins on the appropriate evening, cooking the dinner, cleaning the toilet: these mundane and routine parts of marriage continue, despite your separation. In a situation where you are both, for whatever reason, remaining in the home, it is helpful to clarify these expectations. Having a conversation about practical matters helps to create a clear space for future conversations. Perhaps consider writing down the answers if you are finding it difficult to communicate, so that you are both able to refer to the agreements you made.

Sleeping arrangements may be the most significant change due to separation. One person may move out of the shared bedroom. Again, it is helpful to discuss why this is happening, something we did not do, and what the implications and expectations are as a result. There may be certain rules that need to be followed. For example, if you have decided that your marriage is over and are living together but in separate rooms, it may not be appropriate to bring dates back to the marital home. Perhaps think over how you would feel it is appropriate to behave yourself first or adopt the behaviour you would wish to be displayed towards you.

In some instances, it may be appropriate to offer care for the other person, for example, if they are disabled or unwell. This said, it is good to be aware of the potential of taking on a "parental" role. Are you cooking for them and doing their laundry, while they live in the house as a hotel – as I realized I was doing – or do they need particular help and support?

When May's ex-husband suffered scarring and brain damage, she set up professional carers to spend some time with her husband while she went to work. During their separation and after they divorced, she set boundaries like sleeping in a different room. She continued to liaise with his carers and helped when she could. May said, "It was difficult with his family as they didn't understand his care needs. I attended courses at Headway [the brain injury association[8]] and my husband also got very involved volunteering there."

---

8   www.headway.org.uk/

Questions to consider

What responsibilities are you continuing to take on?

What responsibilities are you hoping your ex-spouse or partner will continue to take on?

What are your expectations of their behaviour while you are separated but living together?

What are your expectations of your own behaviour while you are separated but living together?

Are these the same? If not, consider where you have given leeway or taken advantage of their goodwill and whether this is fair or appropriate.

The length of time you feel able to live in this situation is also worth considering. What seems reasonable now, may in six months' time feel like a thankless situation that is wearing you down. Consider having times to reconnect and look at these questions again. For example, if a condition of living together is to attend weekly counselling, are you both sticking to that?

Moving out

This is perhaps one of the most brutal moments. If you are the person moving out, it creates a raft of questions: Where will I live? How will I pack? What will I take? How can I afford it?

In many ways, moving out provides a new opportunity. It is a new space, devoid of memories, but that space has to be located first and may not be ideal. It may be that in moving out, you feel you have escaped from a horrible situation or have actually escaped from an unhealthy marriage.

Deciding where to go can be daunting. Moving back in with parents may provide financial and emotional security while feeling like a backward step. Moving in with friends can provide a security and support network yet be a daily reminder of the life you used to have and now don't. Living alone can feel like freedom or exacerbate feelings of loneliness. Deciding where to live may depend on your financial situation and whether you can afford a small flat of your own, or whether you will need to lodge with others.

In the Lucy Dillon book *A Hundred Pieces of Me*, a woman chooses which one hundred things from her previous life to bring to her new, smaller home. Some have particular importance for her, but some also for them as a couple. I found it quite liberating when I moved and got rid of a number of things I didn't want or like!

If you have moved out of the marital home or are about to do so, you may have to make quick decisions about what to take or leave, and where to go. These are not easy choices. You will find you can live without things you once thought were vital. There will also be other things that you miss, want and perhaps resent not having with you. The value of these will not necessarily be financial.

If one of you decides to move out, it is important to consider the legal standpoint that may later arise in your divorce proceedings, and you may need to consult a solicitor. It is also important to remember that if both your names are on a mortgage, you are both obliged to keep up repayments, even if you are not living there.

When my ex moved out, he took very few things with him. When we finally decided (about a year later) to divorce, I had been living in the house for a considerable time alone. But I needed to remove everything that was his from the space, in almost a cleansing process. I asked that I be the one to pack his things, that he would then be able to collect. I said I would not be able to help him move his belongings out. The prospect of him coming into what was now my safe space filled me with anxiety.

I chose to pack up his possessions and to be home when he collected them. The thought of him coming to pick up his belongings while I was out, made me feel my privacy and security would be compromised. This is in no way to suggest I ever felt in danger or threatened by him – that was never the case. The space had simply evolved to feel like mine, so his presence in what I now considered "my" home without me felt invasive. Going through these things was painful, but it was helpful to me to see them physically removed. The day he moved his belongings out has stayed in my mind though. I refused to help; he had declined to bring any assistance, and I had roped my mum in to be there as moral support. It was a hard day for all of us. For me, the protection of the space I had begun to feel safe in was essential, and I appreciated that he recognized that and didn't insist on packing his things up with me being there or else being there alone to move things out.

Questions to consider

If you are moving out, where will you move to?

Would it be preferable to live with others or alone?

Are you able to collect belongings?

Will you need to return your key?

How will this impact your divorce from a legal perspective?

How did the division of assets occur?

Carol: He already had his flat and I had my house. A colleague bought out his share of our remaining business – most of which went to pay off debt he had. He had already kept all the deposit on our last joint house purchase, as it was in his name due to my bad credit caused by his spending all the money on alcohol and other things, and me building up credit card debt for food and other bills. He didn't really get the marriage vow thing and why he was still in the house albeit in the spare room – and I felt sorry for him as he wasn't earning much on a business he had set up after we had sold another of the businesses. He had also let his flat and not given himself time to find somewhere else. I realize now that he had manipulated me to move back in with me so I would take care of the bills and he could spend his money how he liked… it was only supposed to be for a few weeks initially.

Decobe: Apart from a few items of furniture she didn't want, I left the home with my own personal items only. There were too many painful memories in that home and I didn't want anything that reminded me of them. I realized that I would need some furniture in any future home so just took the cast-offs to start me in my new life. Surprisingly, I still have those same items of furniture.

May: Due to my ex having a disability, his needs trumped all in spite of his own accident compensation, which was not enough to support his expensive requirements. This made me very depressed as I would be giving up a lot that my late parents had left me. The marital home, at this stage, was still for sale. The barrister in court suggested a number of properties I could move to with the meagre sum allocated to me, to a town outside London where I knew no one. One barrister said I was making a loss at painting and that I should work full time instead of part time. The second barrister (my ex changed barristers partway through the process) said I hadn't put all my artwork on my website so I wasn't selling enough of it.

I had to negotiate a deal in courtrooms to try to keep what I could of my own savings and inherited assets, which were not ring fenced due to my husband's disability and his inability to work more than part time.

We made an inventory of the household things with my ex's case manager present, who mediated between us, as to who would have which furniture or which gifts or inherited items, regardless of to whom they were left or gifted. It helped to have a mediator and something firm written down.

Rowena: He had bought a house, which was rented out while we were living abroad, so I moved into that. He pretty much signed it over to me and bought a car for me. As I would have a claim on his army pension and future income, I think he just wanted a clean break, and it was easier for him to do that.

If you are moving out of the marital home...

- *Would you prefer to pack your own belongings or would you be happy for your ex to do so?*
- *Will you take someone with you to pack?*
- *Will you be willing for your ex to be present?*
- *Is there a mutually acceptable third party who may help you?*
- *What is the time frame for your move? Share this clearly and considerately.*
- *How will you transport your belongings?*

If your ex is moving out of the marital home...

- *Will you be present when they move their belongings out?*
- *If not, how will you cope with their belongings being entirely absent on returning to the space?*

- *Is it acceptable that they are in the space alone?*
- *Is there a mutually acceptable third party who could be present instead?*
- *Will you physically assist them?*
- *Will you assist them in allowing convenient access?*
- *Do you expect them to provide the boxes?*

If you are both moving out...

- *Who is leaving the space first?*
- *Will you pack together?*
- *Will you have previously agreed ownership of particular items or will you do this on the day?*
- *Who will organize any key handovers or will this be done separately?*

Consider your ex's viewpoint

- *These are their belongings, and they may not wish you to go through them, particularly as your relationship has now changed.*
- *They may wish to say "goodbye" to the space.*
- *It may be their home now, and your presence may make their privacy feel invaded.*
- *If you or they have entered a new relationship, consider whether this person's presence is appropriate.*
- *Be mindful of their time schedule – endeavour to be considerate of their job, commitments, and time in your requests.*

Remaining in the marital home

Remaining in the marital home may mean a necessary re-imagining of the space. The absence, or presence, of an object can trigger emotional pain. In remaining in the home, albeit one that has irrevocably changed, you are in familiar surroundings.

I would regularly come across my ex-spouse's guitar plectrums. They were a concrete reminder that once he had been there – and now he was gone. Removing certain objects from my eyeline was incredibly helpful. I put them into the spare room, into "his" bedside table or into a cupboard. It wasn't that I needed to be rid of them: I simply needed to not see them every day.

At every stage of readjusting to my former marital space, I roped in a friend or family member. If I needed to move things, pack things, or sort through things, I called them in. They didn't have to do anything; I just wanted someone there. Having cried a lot on my own, their presence was a comfort, and often an opportunity to laugh in one of the bleakest times of life. Emily, my friend since we were age three, came to help me choose tiles, made me a kitchen blind, and was a regular help with the practical downsizing and redecoration tasks. Her presence helped me to feel less alone in the responsibility of choice. And actually, I enjoyed these choices. Being able to make decisions about where to put things or what to have out on display was empowering. I enjoyed having the pick of bathroom tiles and kitchen blinds myself as it was a positive decision I was able to make – not entirely alone, but with the ultimate choice being mine.

Question to consider

Is there something in your home you find particularly upsetting or difficult to see regularly? If so, consider moving it to a "safe" place.

Financial separation

Aside from physical separation, there may be financial commitments to consider and reassign. At times, I felt extremely angry when money was spent (entirely legitimately) from the joint account, that – because we weren't living together – I hadn't been told about. There is the fear that the other person could "clean you out"; perhaps you've been tempted to do this yourself for some sort of recompense.

Try to honour your financial commitments, especially those that need to be made together. It could be that you need to seek financial advice in order to maintain and fairly apportion financial commitments.

Be accountable to one another, and perhaps also to a trusted friend, for the money you are spending. My most frivolous purchase was a pair of new work trousers. I'd lost a lot of weight so I did need them, but in my heart I'd spent the money because I felt I was entitled to it. But money was only ever going to make me comfortable; it wouldn't make me happy. So, because I knew that every time he spent money and I didn't know what it was for I felt cross, I resolved to improve my own behaviour, and suggested we check with one another for impulse or personal purchases over £25, which we agreed upon.

If your separation has happened suddenly, it can have large implications for your finances. Being left with a single salary, or no salary, will be frightening and require a concentrated effort to re-establish spending patterns: three years on from financial separation, I can often still live with the same mentality as when I had two salaries at my disposal. It is crucial to establish how your finances will now proceed. There is no right or wrong answer to this. You may wish to continue having a joint account for some time, as you are both paying the mortgage and bills. You may feel that sharing an account increases tension and worry, so separating the accounts is wiser. It is important to remember that if both names are on financial documents, you both bear the responsibility for paying the bills, mortgage, and debts. Taking the opportunity to list all your income and expenditure means you will have a clear idea of what you need to do, but when the latter is greater than the former, there is a fear and worry around how you will cope.

Meeting with a financial expert from your bank or a mortgage advisor may help you to transition into your new financial state. You may be able to take a mortgage "holiday" to balance living costs. The bank may be able to waive charges you have accrued or find a higher interest account in which to place your money. Seek out those around you who often manage to get good deals on insurance and ask them to help you find cheaper alternatives. CAP, mentioned earlier, offer free courses on managing money and can even work with you to calculate repayment of creditors and prioritizing your money for living costs.

Questions to consider

Is your money safe? If you are concerned, arrange an urgent appointment with your bank, mortgage advisor, or solicitor.

What were the principles on which you agreed to share your money? Do you need to reiterate these to one another?

How will you honour those principles?

List all your income and expenditure. Who will pay the rent/mortgage, and insurances on any shared properties?

Can you establish a handover of financial responsibilities and work out a realistic time frame for this?

How did you work through the financial cost and implications of divorce?

Carol: Luckily I had some money from my house sale so I could afford to pursue the divorce. I found a fantastic solicitor who offered a fixed fee. The finances were discussed at mediation to save the costs of hiring a barrister. Had that not been the case, on paper I would probably still be married.

Decobe: Once I had a financial sum for my share of the marital home, which I wasn't totally happy with but nevertheless accepted, and it was in my new bank account, that was the end of it.

May: I paid monthly for solicitors' fees so that it didn't mount up. I never counted the total bill as it was too depressing because it was so expensive. I felt that I would rather pay a solicitor than leave money to my ex to spend on other women. I needed my life back and would have to pay to get it, so it was part of survival. I was aware that other people were worse off than me.

Rowena: I got a job almost immediately back in the UK and a friend moved in with me and paid rent.

Chapter Seven

Family

Family ties

When you separate or divorce, sometimes one of the largest senses of loss is related to the extended family you were part of that is yours no longer. Not only have you lost a best friend, a spouse, and a companion, you have potentially lost their extended family and friends network too. Even if these relationships still exist, they may well be altered because of events.

The chances are, we spent time building relationships between two families which now seem to have gone to waste. We may feel that the time we invested in that person and their family has been thrown back in our face, and that the relationship we pursued was pointless as it has all come to nothing. Working out how these relationships can end well or continue is complex.

It may be that you wish to curtail all communication with your ex-spouse's family. You may wish to continue as though nothing has happened in your relationships with their family. Furthermore, if you have children, your spouse's family will likely still be involved in their lives.

Of course, each individual will have their own relationships with the other's close relations and friends. The fact that these relationships will likely have stemmed from one spouse originally does not mean that they have jurisdiction over them. Members of my own family were friends with my ex-husband. These friendships existed outside of our marriage. They would contact one another, spend time together, and enjoy each other's company away from me. When we separated, I encouraged this to continue. I did not feel threatened by their closeness; in fact, I felt our sense of family was strengthened because of it – and I hoped that if these friendships continued, so would our marriage. Years on from our initial separation, I still feel a sense of sadness that these particular friendships were affected by our split.

Allowing your ex and family to maintain or end relationships outside of your marriage may feel like further betrayal of all that you had built together, as they seem to continue to love those people despite not loving you. Or it may feel that they have also rejected them, magnifying your own experience of rejection. In the same way that we cannot control the way our ex behaves or feels, we cannot control their relationships with those around us. Giving "permission" to those around you to continue pursuing the friendship may be a way to avoid the experience of rejection. This does have its own difficulties though: knowing they may well discuss you and your marriage can feel as complicated and troubling as them not discussing it. Even if we can't discuss this with our ex, we can have these conversations with those close to us about the relationship that they might maintain. It may help to reassure ourselves of our own friendships and family relationships, and rejoice in them by doing fun activities together and sharing with one another.

We may also find that certain relationships end. You might have to respect this, as difficult as it can be. Being clear with your spouse that you will be explaining to these people why this relationship is ending seems entirely justified. Your interaction may be no more than a phone call, or a brief face-to-face conversation, because while you will be respecting their wishes, you are also ending well and keeping doors open for future contact. After the initial pain of separation has faded, the relationship may be able to exist once more. To end well may mean that despite a tumultuous friendship between the two of you, you are able to thank them for their involvement in your life or to wish them well. Ending these relationships badly because we are glad to be rid of them is likely to leave an even more bitter taste than the end of the marriage has already left.

Questions to consider

Which of your relationships and friendships do you feel stem from your spouse originally?

Which would you like or hope to maintain? Are there others you feel it necessary or helpful to maintain?

If these relationships need to come to an end, or you would prefer they did, is there a way to end them well?

Are there relationships your spouse has with your family or friends that you may find difficult?

Mourning the loss of your ex-spouse's family and friends may be as vital a component as mourning your relationship's end. Giving yourself time and permission to do this is helpful too.

In-laws

You might love your in-laws, but primarily they are your spouse's parents. This means that their first loyalties are most likely to be to their child, regardless of what they may have done to lead to the marital breakdown. While incredibly painful and possibly justifiably angering – this is healthy and right: of course, a parent will want to protect their child. Decades of time spent together will have established relationships and ways of working between them that we have forever been outsiders to. However much we felt we understood it, we may find that it has played out differently to how we expected, or even if it is exactly as we anticipated, we will not know what is said behind closed doors.

Their loyalty may then dictate the state of their communication with you. Perhaps they are angry at you, justifiably or not, because of their overriding love for their child. Perhaps they are embarrassed or ashamed of their child's actions, but are expressing that through distancing themselves from you, unsure of how to behave. It may feel that their rejection of you is the last in a long line of things you seem to have done "wrong" and you are relieved at the prospect of never needing to see them again. These suggestions are of course merely conjecture. Without full and frank discussion, we can never know what they are feeling and why they may have chosen to remain close to us or to distance themselves. But first we must acknowledge the pain that any rejection of the relationship causes.

I regarded myself as my in-laws' daughter. They welcomed me into their family and loved me. I endeavoured to include my mother-in-law in as many things as I could, particularly "female-only" events, such as wedding dress shopping and the hen party. I stayed in touch with her for quite some time post-divorce while my father-in-law and I didn't communicate. When I messaged him on his birthday some months after the divorce, it became apparent he had deleted my number. I found this mildly painful, and also a bit embarrassing – after all, I had hoped the birthday wishes would be welcomed. I had to choose to let go of that relationship. It was understandable that he had chosen to do so – I was no longer married to his son – and now I needed to do the same, by wishing them well and letting go of any possible further communication with them. I wrote to my in-laws to thank them for their investment in me and our marriage and to wish them well: I wanted to show them I still valued them, regardless of the state of the relationship between their son and me.

It may be that we need to choose to forgive our in-laws for pain that they have caused us, in the same way we may need to forgive an ex-spouse. Forgiveness will of course be a much harder prospect if you have felt sidelined, hurt, or rejected by your in-laws. The process of forgiving them for decisions they have made, regardless of what those were, will take time, and may need to be a daily choice. As the ex-spouse though, we can also choose to honour that familial allegiance, in the same way we might hope our own family would fight our corner. Their parents, rightly or wrongly in our eyes, love them, and want to protect them regardless of situation or choice. By choosing to respect that familial love and bond, we may find forgiveness can extend to the wider family members.

On one area of communication there is a reasonably clear line though: extolling your ex-spouse's failings to their family is unlikely to bring about the result of making the family angry with them. The protection of those close to us is often innate, and will be the primary reaction, even while we disagree with what they have done. Imagine your own child, sibling, or parent: if they have done something wrong and someone justifiably points out all their flaws, chances are your natural reaction will be to protect, even while storing up the things to tell them later! Choosing to express your anger, loss, and hurt to your in-laws will not necessarily bring about a united front of you and your in-laws versus your ex. If you choose to share the facts, it is worth asking your ex to speak to them, even if you are present, to ensure the truth is given.

If you have children it may be necessary to establish lines of communication. Erik Castenskiold's book *Restored Lives: Recovery from Divorce and Separation* is incredibly helpful in offering guidance on this topic. Primarily, putting the feelings of all adult parties aside in order to offer full communication, support, and love between grandparent and grandchild may be what is needed. Other communication between the adults may then need to take a secondary place to the wellbeing of the child and also to take place outside of the communication about the familial contact. Your spouse may wish to cut all contact between you and their family. As discussed before, no one can preclude anyone else from friendship, but it may be possible to inform your ex-in-laws of this and to encourage healthy relationships regardless, by taking an interest in what your child does while with this side of the family. Having no contact while they are there may also prove difficult, so establishing ground rules and means of communication wherever possible will be necessary. Again, Castenskiold's book and the Restored Lives course provide constructive ways to approach this. Although it is a Christian course run by UK churches, as with CAP there is no obligation to be of that, or any, faith to take part.

Questions to consider

How have your in-laws reacted?

Has their reaction surprised you in any way?

How did you see your relationship with them? Is it something you hope to continue, are willing to grieve, or are relieved to see the end of?

How did you manage the separation from, or continuing relationship with, your in-laws?

Carol: We didn't see them that often while we were married so it wasn't too difficult. I did send Christmas cards etc. for a couple of years and his mum always sent me an Easter card. More difficult was not seeing my stepson – however, he is now in his late 20s and I have a good relationship with him. He has been let down badly by other adults in his life, and I am the only significant parental figure in his life that he can truly trust.

Decobe: I had a very good relationship with my in-laws, as I suppose they regarded me as a son, to replace their own adult son who had been killed a few years earlier. At the time of the divorce only my father-in-law was still surviving. So we both carried on as before, and I always regularly visited "Dad" when down in the West Country where he lived (my own father having already passed away). I think he initially found the situation difficult but within a few visits he had come to terms with the situation and always welcomed me in for a hug and a cuppa, followed by a long chat.

Ellie: This was difficult because I was very much part of his family and he was part of mine, so the relationship breakdown was painful for everyone. I initiated seeing my in-laws once while we were separated because I wanted them to know the truth about what was going on. However, I knew that regardless of what had happened, their loyalty was to him, so they couldn't be there for me. If we had got back together I know they would have been supportive but once the divorce was initiated, I didn't feel it was appropriate to see them, even though part of me wanted to. For a long time I felt really sad and it seemed very unfair that other relationships I valued had to end, again not from my choosing. I missed his family, but now looking back I realize that it was an important part of being able to move on.

Rowena: Apart from one conversation with one of his sisters, I never saw or heard from any of them again. They lived in Scotland, so they were miles away. They didn't try and keep in contact.

Life events and invitations

As I approached thirty, eighteen months after my divorce was finalized, I decided to have an enormous party. Parties, in my experience, had mainly revolved around birthdays and weddings, and as I wasn't getting married I decided this was as good an excuse as any to eat a lot of food and have a dance. But I floundered over who to invite. It was to be a large party: a mixture of family and friends. A particular stumbling block I encountered was whether I invited a relation's ex-wife with whom I got on well to a family function. I invited my relative and then waited. Having not heard from him, time quickly disappeared and I left it too long to issue an invitation to his ex. This bothered me for some time afterwards. The woman in question is lovely. I have had frank chats with both halves about their marriage. They have children whom I see sometimes. What was the ideal way forward?

This is not an uncommon problem. As families divide in divorce, the issuing of invitations and people's presence at life events becomes considerably more complex. Firstly, there is the question of whether the divorcing couple are amicable – both willing and able to be around one another – and then there are the wider relationships around the couple too. Other members of my family attended the party, and there would have been their relationships with his newly ex-wife to consider too. But perhaps that was not my decision to make, much as it was not really any of my business. I like both parties in the previous relationship: could I have invited them both and let them know the other was also invited so that they could liaise? Could this have caused difficulties for them, though? Perhaps asking my family member if he minded his ex-wife being invited would have been acceptable, or courteously letting him know I had done so? There was no clear way to proceed, and the difficulty is that there isn't a clear structure or rule for these events: the feeling of divided loyalty is a peculiar one. But perhaps, as we may experience, the opportunity to politely decline is more helpful, because having been invited we then feel wanted, loved, and included, regardless of circumstances.

There is a contrasting challenge when you are not invited to an event in your ex-spouse's family. That can feel like a painful snub and rejection once again from people you used to be close to. Choosing not to take this as a deeply personal omission is difficult; you may have been close to them and been part of the preparation for the event. Wishing them well is still possible – as is offering to celebrate with them separately if they have voiced complications over the invitation process. As we have seen, being forced to choose where one's loyalties lie is not easy for family members either, so our gracious response if we receive an invitation, unless offence has been consciously spoken about to you by the event holder, is a gift we can offer them.

Questions to consider

How do you feel about being left out of familial events?

Are there ways you could celebrate these events separately?

Are you able to ask whether your former spouse has been invited?

Carol's story

I was brought up in an "average" family with my mum, dad, and sister. Dad is not a churchgoer. He struggles with a God who, in his view, allows so many bad things to happen. Mum was a Christian all her life with a very strong faith. She was a Sunday school teacher and we had to go every week. In those days church was old-fashioned and not child-friendly! She told us once we were confirmed we could make up our own minds. We got confirmed and promptly never went again!

My faith was confirmed as being misplaced when I went on a school cruise and it was pointed out that all the miracles, such as the tearing of the temple curtain, could be explained by science and natural disasters (though I later realized that the miracle was in the precise timing). I think I had always believed in God, but I came back to faith when I moved house and did an Alpha course. I was baptized in 1999.

I met my ex-husband at a new job in 1993. I saw him walking down the road with a colleague and kind of fell in love a little bit! We were both in relationships but remained friends for five years. We finally got together in the summer of 1999. He proposed on Christmas Eve in 1999 after Midnight Mass, and he gave his life to Jesus at a Millennium party we went to with our church friends. He started talking about having a family, and we started a business together. He basically delivered everything I wanted on a plate. I was thirty-seven when we married in May 2000.

Everything changed on our wedding day. He got drunk and left our room on our wedding night to go and see his best man, so our marriage was not consummated. Our honeymoon in Israel was booked for two weeks starting the following Thursday, so in the meantime we went to North Devon. He got drunk again and went out without me, coming back in the middle of the night with two girls in tow, saying they needed somewhere to stay! I told them where to go in no uncertain terms. It turned out he was an alcoholic and womanizer. It also turned out that he didn't want a family, and his way of preventing that from happening was to not have sex.

It was a disaster, but I had made my vows. He didn't drink every day, but every few weeks he would go on a binge and disappear for a weekend. He lost his wedding ring during one of those weekends. I finally left and moved in with my parents, but he got in trouble with the police and they would only release him on bail if I was there, so I ended up moving back in. We separated again when I found out that he was having a physical affair.

I forgave him, took him back, and cancelled the divorce I had started, but on the condition that we had counselling. This offered him the psychological help he needed and it was beginning to work. However, the final nail in the coffin was an emotional affair he was having with another lady, which had been going on even while he was having the physical affair. When I asked him to stop all contact with her, he blamed her. He refused to send a solicitor's letter, and in a final counselling session refused to change his phone number. As he was putting his friendship with her above my feelings I had nowhere to go except divorce.

Many people questioned why I cancelled the divorce the first time and took him back. My answer is that I understood his issues stemmed from his childhood, and if he could have sorted these out things would have been OK. Unfortunately, when the counselling started tackling the issues that led to the drinking and womanizing he stopped going.

I took my marriage vows seriously, regardless of whether he honoured his or not, and had married him "in sickness and in health". If I had ended the marriage sooner I wouldn't have felt I had done my utmost to make it work. When I finally divorced him, I knew that I could move on with a clear conscience, confident there was nothing else I could have done. The one sadness I have is that the opportunity to have a child was not left in God's hands but was taken away by my husband. I do have a wonderful stepson, though.

Chapter Eight

Your Ex-spouse or Partner

Staying in touch

Are there *any* good ways to stay in touch? As I pondered this during our divorce proceedings as it approached my ex-husband's birthday, a friend asked me how I'd feel if I *didn't* get in touch. Would I be more comfortable getting in touch politely, or remaining silent and letting the relationship conclude through our lack of contact? So, on his birthday as our divorce went through the courts, I texted him. I didn't want him to feel that I was bitter, and I did want him to have a good day. I wasn't planning on sending a card or a present, but a polite message wishing him a good day felt appropriate in the circumstances. The following year, I didn't text: our divorce had been finalized and we didn't have any contact unless there was a specific need. That particular door, I felt, had closed. He was welcome to enjoy his birthday thoroughly, but I was in no way involved and our lives were closed to one another; he was becoming more and more of a stranger as time progressed. It is an odd feeling when someone you were so close to becomes someone you don't know at all, so to remodel the relationship without that depth and intensity takes tact, patience, and a letting go of all entitlement to their innermost thoughts and feelings.

Where communication was necessary, a strategy I employed was to conduct it through media such as email. Email meant I could respond at a later point without the speedy reply often expected in texts or the aptly named "instant" messages. As well as this, email allowed many more words to explain situations and nuance. I changed the ringtones on my phone for his name so that I would be fully aware if he was texting or calling me, and not feel constant nerves and apprehension whenever my phone went off – especially in the early days when things felt very confusing and unsettled. I also put the letter "X" in front of his name to avoid accidentally messaging or calling him when I was scrolling through my contacts. It wasn't the fact he was my ex, so much as the lack of anyone else with a name beginning with the letter x in my life!

If children are involved in your separation or divorce, you are likely to need much more contact, but it is worth considering the ways in which you communicate. Perhaps you always speak on the phone so there can be no misinterpretation of tone, or via email to ensure everything is clearly written down. If you do not have children, then your involvement with one another may naturally conclude as your divorce proceedings do. Once again, there's not a right or a wrong decision.

In what ways did you most effectively communicate with your former spouse?

Carol: We communicated by phone or text and email about work, as for a while he helped out with the business. It helped that we didn't and don't hate each other. I actually feel a bit sorry for him as he has issues from his past which he has never dealt with, and which led to his alcoholism and womanizing.

Decobe: Mostly, at the time, through my solicitor, or the very rare brief phone call. She had made it clear she wanted no part of me, nor I her – such was the state of emotions at that time.

Ellie: We mostly talked face to face, which I found the most useful way of communicating. I think it's helpful to take non-verbal communication and tone of voice into account when you're discussing something so personal and important. Even so, at the beginning our conversations seemed to go round and round in circles, which was frustrating, and his explanation was quite muddled at times. I found it reassuring when some close friends met up with him and said they found the same. When my ex-husband moved out I told him I wasn't going to contact him for a while because I felt that during the process he had been treating me a bit like a girlfriend, which wasn't fair. I was clear that I would either be his wife, or otherwise not part of his life at all. I didn't contact him for about six weeks and it was incredibly difficult not to (although it helped that I dropped my phone down the loo and broke it!) but I felt he needed to know I meant it and to consider the consequences.

Rowena: We did meet up and talk. Mobile [cell] phones weren't invented then, so we spoke occasionally on the landline, but mainly we met in person.

Managing your ex's emotions

One of the most agonizing things about relationship breakdown is that the very person you want to share all the pain, difficulties, and thought processes with, is the one person you can't speak to. Conversely, they may expect you to continue to be there for them and to be the sounding board for their feelings and emotions, even while holding you at a distance in terms of your marriage relationship. As Ellie described earlier, clarifying that this won't be the case and sticking to it is extremely difficult, but ultimately helpful and worth it.

Processing the emotions of the past and future together can be very helpful, and naturally the less a couple communicates, the more distant they will become. Sharing your emotions and stance with one another is a positive step in opening opportunities to reconcile; yet when reconciliation is not a realistic prospect, it is also important to build in a distinction between your marriage and the new relationship that will now exist between you. If they have chosen to leave, it is not your responsibility to become their sounding board and it is equally not their prerogative to ask you personal questions about your life. The transition from best friends and lovers to strangers is a hugely difficult one to negotiate. While being "cagey" about your life feels unnatural, it also means you are working things through for yourself, finding other support networks, and it is the beginning of moving on.

After we decided to divorce, I chose to also change career (this isn't compulsory!) As we moved further apart and saw each other less throughout the divorce, I found it increasingly challenging to answer questions about my job applications and new role. While circumstances dictated we still saw each other occasionally, I became protective of my new life. I felt it was not his business any longer. Through asking, it felt like he wanted to show he cared. However, to me he wasn't willing to care in the ways I felt mattered as husband and wife. By having a new situation and not disclosing information and details about it, I was also becoming my own individual person with a separate life: a life he was no longer part of. It had taken me a long time – years! – to accept that and to move on to the situation I was then in, so protecting that became important in defining the new relationship. I may not have wanted it, but I was going to make the best of it. I found a helpful way to do this was not to enquire about his life and allowing that to become a separate life from my own too. I answered his questions politely, vaguely, and without revealing any particular details.

However, in distancing myself from my ex, I also asked particular friends to keep me updated. I asked them to tell me if he got a new partner, had a child, or moved house or job. The prospect of, for example, being chatty and pleasant in the supermarket to him and a new pregnant partner was harrowing. I didn't want to know all about what he was doing day-to-day, but to be aware of any major life changes meant I would not be suddenly faced with an awkward situation and a flood of unexpected emotions. To ask about these things was a safeguard for me, helping me to avoid social media stalking, knowing friends would keep me informed. This gradually became less of a problem, to the point where I am no longer curious about what his life is like now, other than to hope he has forgiven himself and found happiness too. This wasn't somewhere I expected to be six years ago, so don't worry if you're not there yet! There is no set time frame and no expectation to be "there" at a certain point. For some it may happen quickly; for others it may take more than six years.

Questions to consider

Are you managing your ex's emotions about your separation and divorce in a healthy way?

Are you sharing these together? Is your ex simply listening to you without responding, or are you listening to your ex without them listening to you?

Are there parts of your life you can begin to establish as separate if you are heading towards divorce and separate lives?

Physical intimacy with your ex

If you were of a generation who watched *Friends*, you may remember the episode of Monica and Chandler's engagement – "The One with

Monica's Thunder". In it, Rachel, wrestling feelings of joy for her best friend and inner turmoil over her own unknown relationship future, suggests to Ross that they have a "bonus night". Ross jumps at the chance, as – for those uninitiated in the term – bonus night is a night of no-strings-attached sex with someone you've previously had a sexual relationship with, outside of the relationship commitment. Rachel and Ross had never taken this opportunity, and this kind of physical comfort was exactly what Rachel, understandably, felt she needed.

Now you may be thinking, "*Great!* I could do with this right now." And no one would blame you, least of all me. The scene of someone else's relationship joy and their clear delight in their other half is a situation bound to stir up a yearning within you for that familiar intimacy. Ross and Rachel's previous relationship would have meant they would know the score: they'd know the familiarity of making love with one another and, granted, everyone would probably have enjoyed themselves at the time. But the challenge of "bonus night" was already implicit before it became a reality (I won't spoil the episode for you): the age-old question – what would this mean? What implications would it have? And it's this question that we have to be acutely aware of as we separate and divorce, in the midst of a time when we want comfort and support like no other.

Your other half will have seen you at the best of times and the worst of times. They've seen you dressed up on your wedding day and ill, unable to leave the bathroom. They know what you look like with no clothes on; there's nothing new there – and if your main incentive to make love is so they can see your new muscular physique, washboard stomach, or newly purchased underwear, stop right there!

Where familiarity can breed contempt, it can also be the biggest of comforts. So the comfort of knowing who, what, when, and how is a huge draw. The physical comfort of being close to another person, with whom you're so familiar, is profound. But there's a problem with bonus night – several actually, as Rachel and Ross discover – so it's good to consider these before we engage in physical intimacy with our ex.

What are we expressing?

Maybe you are expressing your love for the person in the giving of your body to them, and in giving them pleasure. Maybe you are simply looking to fulfil your sexual desire in a way that seems appropriate – after all, you're both married consenting adults.

So first we should consider, what are our motives?

Questions to consider

What does a kiss mean to you? Does it signify love? Is it a habit?

What does anything more than that mean? Is it an expression of love or to gratify sexual desires?

Why do you want to make love with your ex? Why do they want to do this? Is it for a physical connection, emotional connection, to satisfy their desire, or to fulfil your own needs?

Are you choosing your needs and desires over theirs? If this is to fulfil something in you, consider whether that is serving them well, but also whether you are serving yourself well in choosing this.

It may be useful to talk this over with a counsellor or a trusted friend. It's a difficult subject to bring up, but there is great accountability in it. Ask them to ask you these questions and discuss what your truthful answers are. These may change, and that's to be expected

– we do not stay the same for ever. Answering these questions helped me to clarify what my own ideas and motives were and to understand that what *I* felt was expressed in a kiss, was not necessarily what he intended to express to me. Kissing one another goodbye wasn't particularly helpful, as it led me to believe there was love and the possibility of reconciliation where there was none.

Reflect on the emotions that are at the forefront of your heart too. Are you looking to boost your self-esteem because they won't be able to resist you physically? Are you looking to hurt them by leaving after because you're angry? Are you hoping they will want to stay because of the physical enjoyment you will both have experienced? Consider whether bitterness, low self-esteem, desperation, or any other emotions you may be experiencing might be impacting your judgment.

Consider your own motives carefully. The passage from 1 Corinthians 13 about love is often read at weddings. Even at this point, we could consider whether what we are doing is acting in accordance with this love, or in order to hurt our ex-spouse.

What do we think they are expressing?

We can't psychoanalyse someone from afar – and I'm not suggesting this would be a good option. But if their expectations aren't explicitly the same as yours, one or both of you could be hurt and further pained by the experience.

Asking them what their intentions or expressions are may be necessary – and while it may sound like a mood-killer, doing so will alleviate the "second guessing" and confusion that could otherwise surround these expressions of intimacy. A mood-killer may be necessary. If you choose to hold on to the connection of sex between you, consider whether they and you are also willing to invest emotionally, spiritually, and practically in the pursuit of your marriage, as well as continuing a physical relationship.

Isn't sex good for marriage though?

Yes! I would wholeheartedly agree that sex is good for marriage – it's great! And depending on the status of your marriage, it may be entirely appropriate to continue building and experiencing that physical, emotional, and spiritual closeness that can come through sexual intimacy. But if your marriage is experiencing difficulties, it may be worth considering the above questions together, and explaining what making love means to you and what you feel you are expressing through those actions.

When your ex-spouse's life moves on

"I want him to be happy… I just want me to be happier."

Charming as it is, this was my summary to one of my brothers about my perspective on happiness. It wasn't that I wanted my ex-husband to have an unhappy life; I was happy for him to be happy. But I wanted to know that I was somehow happier, had achieved slightly more and had reached these dreams first. This is not the attitude of a gracious, forgiving ex-wife. It is, however, the honest, real-life attitude of an ex-wife.

Dealing with divorce encompasses facing up to the dreams that will never be realized: perhaps having children; perhaps sitting lovingly together in the future at your child's wedding; holidays; houses you hoped to buy – there are the big dreams, and the tiny ones. If you are looking at your ex's life and seeing these very dreams happen to them while they are not happening to you, that is hard to bear. It is difficult not to feel jealousy or envy. Even when we see these events happening in the lives of people we perhaps didn't get on as well with at school, or a co-worker who we don't much like but good things seem to happen to, it's hard. When you're replacing that with your own dreams being realized by the person you'd hoped to fulfil them with who is now doing so without you, the difficulty takes on a whole new angle. In many ways anger and envy are justifiable emotions. In marriage we committed to those dreams together. Even if it's something you didn't want it can be difficult too, because they are experiencing what we perceive as success while we are not.

My strangest sense of rivalry came through coming across my ex-husband's website. He was, and I assume still is, a very talented photographer. His website looked excellent (yes, I was stalking). My own blog was looking, well, *fine*, but nothing overly special or dynamic. And I was jealous. I wanted my website to look great, to have funds and time and *skill* to devote to that. I was jealous of what, to my mind, he had had time to do while not looking after a home and a car and holding down an insanely busy job.

An interesting talk I went to a while later sprung a new thought on me when talking about comparison between women: if I was envious of what someone else did, had, or looked like, what was it about that, that I was wanting myself? Was there therefore some way to use that envy to focus my own mind on what I wanted to achieve? I began to ask myself that question about my reaction to my ex-husband. What was it I wanted as I envied his website? Really, I wanted something similarly visually engaging myself. I didn't want his life, his website, or his photographic skill. I wanted an attractive website to make it seem I was successful in my field. More than that, I wanted people to read my blog, to engage with my writing, and to identify with what I had to say in the same way I imagined people engaging with his images. Note that the second part was imagined; I had no idea whether people were indeed engaging, but what I perceived as success was enough for me to become envious.

Difficult as it was, I had to return to key questions. What made me happy about my life? Not in comparison to his, but just because of what I was doing and where I was at. What did I hope to achieve? Was there a way, if I was envious of anything, that I could strive towards that for myself?

In many ways, the example of the website is trivial. When your ex-spouse's life moves on to new relationships, children, jobs, or locations it is extremely difficult not to succumb to envy and bitterness. But we do not want their life. What we seek is our own dream-fulfilling experiences that breathe life into our souls. What the vision of their life reminds us, is that we want these things. Maybe you resent their ready cash-flow while you struggle to make ends meet. Perhaps their life looks carefree while you care single-handedly for your children. Our envy needs to spur us on to capturing what is best in our own lives and driving us forward to achieve those things, rather than winding us up into a spiral of bitterness that leads to resentment.

Questions to consider

What, if anything, do you envy or feel jealous of in your ex-partner's current life?

Why do you feel envious or jealous of these things?

Do these link into your own particular dreams? Is there any way you can work toward your own dream, using this envy as a springboard of inspiration?

Can you be pleased for them? Is there a way you can be happy for them, or forgiving in your attitude towards them?

This philosophical approach to envy can be applied to many of the situations we've talked about throughout this chapter. Sometimes we can do nothing to change anything except our attitude toward others' experiences – but if this is all we can change, there is merit in us striving for love, joy, and contentment through changing the thought processes we have around it.

Chapter Nine

What to Do about Social Media

Making an announcement

Friend. Unfriend. Follow. Unfollow. Block. Mute. Hide posts. Untag. Delete. Surely divorce was easier pre-social media?

It seems unlikely it was any more straightforward, yet the minefield of Facebook, Twitter, and Instagram, to mention a few, is not an easy one to navigate. With life on public display, it can feel imperative to decide on what message to portray as you go public with your separation and divorce. Even if you don't plan a big declaration, deciding on the deletion of friendships, photos, and followings is a complex and emotional decision.

Firstly, you could question whether it is necessary to announce your separation. Sometimes this might feel like the easiest way of letting people know the situation. I used a blog post to reveal both my separation and my new job; this was a substantial amount of time after the actual separation, and I eventually shared on Facebook over a year after that fateful holiday. Those in your close, actual-real-life friend circles will probably already know, so sharing a status might be to stop awkward "Oh, how's your other half?" conversations with anyone else. That said, it's quite simply none of Facebook's or anyone else's business. And it doesn't have to be done straight away.

Letting people know further down the line with a status might feel helpful, but if all those nearby already know it's just a wider public announcement.

Happily, changing one's relationship status can now be done without the big announcement Facebook can feel necessary; a quiet removal of that entry from any sections of information about yourself will suffice. That said, letting people know with as much or as little detail as you want is up to you. A good question to ask yourself might be: what do I mind people knowing? Whatever that is, don't tell them what you don't want them to know – it's your business, not theirs. Give them the bare bones, entire story, or let them work it out from the absence of your spouse; there's no right or wrong, but once it's out there, it's out there. Take some time, draft, definitely don't do it while drunk, and maybe have a friend read it through too. What goes out on the internet is very difficult to retract.

Questions to consider

What do you want the social media world to know?

What would you like it not to know?

Staying friends online

A second question is whether to stay friends online. Maybe it's easier to stay friends online so you can keep tabs on what's going on with them? By the same token, your ex can see what you're doing. Do you want them to see? It can be tempting to portray the perfect "I'm single and fine" photos and great life experiences purely for their perusal. But perhaps it's easier not to pretend.

On the flip side, consider how you will feel if you stumble across their life news too. You're scrolling through your Facebook feed far later at night than you'd intended, when you discover that several, no, tens of your friends have liked the new photo your ex has posted. A happily coupled-up photo on holiday. A family snap – ready made family, several shiny smiles. And you might *know* that it's a veneer – reality doesn't look like that – but right now that doesn't matter. What matters is that they're happy without you, they've moved on, and it hurts.

Again, there's no right or wrong. I found it helpful to unfriend, unfollow, and all the rest of it; my life was no longer connected to his, and to snoop and compare wasn't a healthy or helpful prospect. Instead, I asked a few trusted friends to let me know of any big life changes in his life so that if we accidentally bumped into each other I wouldn't be sideswiped with information. Happily, reasonably quickly, even that wasn't necessary; I was too busy living my own life to worry about his. I did sometimes find it hard not to snoop though. A danger with social media is that it's difficult not to wonder about your ex's life and how they are doing without you, and then be able to easily access that information. Don't beat yourself up if you do end up on a social media stalk at 3 a.m. But do remember it's three in the morning – an unwise time to make big decisions or get in touch because of something you've seen. Just as you are choosing deliberately what to share and what to keep private on social media, they too are presenting a filtered front. Try and keep accountable to a friend about how you're doing with social media stalking. There was nothing on my ex's account about our break-up. I was, I think, hoping to ascertain whether he was still seeing another woman, but as that had never been publicized on social media anyway, I'm not sure what I expected to find. It always threw up more questions and concerns than it ever solved.

If you decide to remain friends, check your own motives for posting too. If it's to make them jealous of your life, consider whether it's worth it. As we present a false front to life it becomes difficult to maintain and can make us feel sadder about where life actually is.

Questions to consider

Do you want to maintain friendship on social media?

What would you be happy for your ex to witness about your life?

Are you posting to arouse jealousy?

Wider friendships on social media

Having deliberated and decided whether to delete or unfriend your ex-spouse, what then about all those other mutual friends? Their parents, siblings, cousins, particular friends – what's the answer here? Again, unfortunately, there's no perfect answer. Are you happy to post or not post and have them see? Is it an important line of communication to keep open?

In some ways I found these decisions were tougher and much less clear-cut than the former. I didn't dislike these people: they weren't horrible – in fact, they had been my family. I loved them. Eventually, I felt that I could no longer feel my life was potentially under scrutiny, even though it may well not have been. I unfriended the majority of his friends and family on my Facebook account. Where the connection to my ex was less close they stayed, and if there were other friendships where social events would bring us together, they stayed too. I did toy with sending a message, but I figured they would understand. There's no right and wrong; your friendship with those people is allowed to exist separately – it's up to you. Just because you're not friends online doesn't mean you can't communicate offline.

This said, as we have already explored, where it isn't up to you is who your ex is friends with. Maybe they follow your best friend, maybe they exchange pleasantries with your family; this isn't your call. If you'd rather not hear about them or see them online choose the appropriate "hide all from" or "mute", and if people insist on sharing details from your ex's life with you, tell them you're not interested, as evidenced by the fact you're no longer following them on accounts. Letting those friendships continue and flourish can be hard to do. But remember – chances are, as you spend gradually less time talking about your ex, they're probably not talking about you either.

Memories on social media

Albums of holidays, being tagged in joint pictures, and the online wedding albums pose a further consideration. Now thanks to Timehop and Facebook we can also take a quick look back over the months leading up to the wedding: events you experienced together and possibly everything being in a former name if you're a woman.

It's important to acknowledge that you can't erase the past. These things happened and deleting the photos doesn't mean they didn't take place. That said, they don't have to serve as a constant reminder on social media. The "memory" function can be a helpful way to systematically untag oneself in the images and allow you to delete any you've taken yourself. It might also be that you prefer to keep some: your life did happen after all. I've had conversations about wedding dresses where people asked me what mine was like. There are a few of my pictures from this time that are set to "private" on my profile picture album, so I can still show them to some friends if I wish to.

You don't have to delete photos because of other people. If someone wants to take the time to scroll back through the annals of your photographic history then they can; chances are that they won't, and if they do, how much do you mind? Maybe you feel more comfortable without them on public display, but want to keep them; maybe you really aren't bothered; or maybe you want to delete the whole lot – all are good decisions.

Ultimately, it might even be that you decide to start anew on social media, setting new boundaries for a new life. There are no rules you have to follow; simply make the decisions that feel right for you.

How did you handle social media in the wake of your separation and divorce?

Carol: I was honest but brief on Facebook: I posted only significant events like my decree nisi and change of name. My ex wasn't on Facebook so I suppose that made it easier.

Decobe: Thankfully, social media did not exist in those days so the problem never arose. Even if they had existed I would not have made use of them. I still refuse to use them today!

Ellie: I personally don't think social media is a place for discussing separation or divorce in the early days – you're much too fragile. My ex-husband deleted his accounts, which meant I didn't need to concern myself with what he was posting or have opportunity to read into things. But it also meant that there was no way for me to see what had been hidden, which I found frustrating at the time but perhaps was for the best. Social media can be a great tool, but when you're feeling vulnerable it's better to avoid posting because you can't take back what you put out there! I don't think saying horrible things makes you feel better, and you need actual support rather than virtual support from friends. "Real life" was, and is, much more important to me. I'm not sure that there are many things like separation and divorce that slap you in the face and wake you up to real life in quite the same way.

May: Once I was divorced I put it on Facebook on my timeline. It was a statement like being born or achieving something or being reborn! Finally I was free, no longer having to tiptoe around my ex and I could officially move out! One of the pastors from our church was concerned about me as he saw it on Facebook and he and his wife were very supportive.

Rowena: It wasn't a thing back then, so I didn't have to deal with any of that. I did find it hard keeping in contact with friends who were good friends with him too, as every time we met, they felt they had to tell me what he was up to. I just wasn't interested, so I let those relationships slide.

Questions to consider

Are there helpful reasons to remain friends on social media?

Who do you want to see if you post about your life? Who do you not want to see?

Will you therefore abstain from social media, or remove your ex as a contact?

Is it helpful to you to announce your separation? How can you do this honestly and fairly, without simply bad-mouthing your ex? Can you ask a trusted friend to read through before you post?

How do you feel about the presence of happier memories on your profiles?

Chapter Ten

What to Do about Wedding Items

Wedding jewellery

Your wedding ring is perhaps one of the most obvious outward signs of your marriage. You may feel that to take off your wedding ring suggests something about your marriage. If someone is committing adultery, they may remove their ring while they are with the third party: a sign that they don't wish to remember their marriage at that point. Removing your wedding ring can therefore feel like an admission that your marriage is not working, is irretrievable, or that you are somehow no longer committed to it.

While wedding rings are a symbol of our love and commitment, they are also just that: a symbol. If you are not wearing your ring, it does not mean you are uncommitted – after all, we may regularly take off rings to wash up, shower, or sleep. The obvious and best answer to the question "When should I take off my wedding ring?" is whenever you feel it's appropriate and you are comfortable to do so. Choosing different options in different situations may feel more realistic. Just because you take your ring off while at home, doesn't mean you must leave it off all the time. At church, for example, where many people knew us both, I would wear my wedding and engagement rings. Initially, after I had moved out, I took them off because I felt that my ex was uncommitted to our marriage, but I would spend the whole time out covering my left hand with my sleeve. Fortunately, it was autumn so this wasn't completely impossible! After a time I simply wore them because wearing them didn't compound the visual evidence of his absence and it avoided questions I couldn't bear to answer. Wearing them also gave a clearer indication of where I was at: I was committed to our marriage and to making it work. While around those I was most comfortable with, though, I would sometimes remove them to put them in my pocket because that felt like a more realistic expression of my life as it was. Because these friends knew the situation, there were no questions around the wearing or non-wearing of the rings.

Removing or wearing your wedding ring may be symbolic of how you feel about the current state of your marriage, but it is not a complete picture. Only you can know how you feel about the wearing of your wedding ring. Is it important to wear it all the time? To what extent does it symbolize your marriage? In the same way, only you will know which contexts you feel happy to wear or to remove it in.

However you feel about your wedding ring, there is no guarantee your spouse feels the same; they may never have worn one. But seeing them and realizing they are not wearing their ring (if they wore one) may be a hugely emotive experience – as it may be for them if you've chosen to remove yours. Before you see them, you may want to consider how you would react if you saw them without their wedding ring on. What do you feel this says? This may also help you to decide whether or not to wear your own ring. Rather than accusing them if this situation arises, it brings the opportunity for discussion. Was there a particular reason one or both of you decided to remove or wear your rings? When you exchanged rings, what was it you said and is this something you are wanting to continue to commit to now?

When I took my engagement and wedding rings off, I knew they no longer held the meaning they once had. The words that were spoken when they were gifted had become obsolete. The love, far more precious than the objects themselves, was no longer being bestowed upon me. The value of the rings, disregarding their beauty, was in the intention of the gift-giver.

Longer term, you might decide you'd like to wear your engagement ring as a beautiful piece of jewellery without the romantic meaning. I felt my rings were beautiful, but the meaning and sentiment behind them no longer existed. For a long time they hung on my jewellery stand, tucked out of the way, but eventually I decided to sell my engagement ring and purchase a brand new piece of jewellery that to me still symbolizes the strength of character I had realized I had. My wedding ring, however, still hangs on that same stand. My plan is to one day give it away, or perhaps come full circle and throw it into the river of the city where our marriage collapsed.

If I had had children, I might have passed any rings on to them as part of their parents' memory. But as I don't, I decided to pass the beauty on to someone else to form new memories, via eBay. Keep it in a drawer, sell it on, wear it – what matters is what feels right for you: there is no right or wrong approach to wearing your wedding jewellery. And it might look different according to the situation. Whatever you do is an individual choice: our rings symbolize things to each of us that even our spouse may not realize. Taking time to make this choice helps: give different things a try and see what feels comfortable and appropriate for the time. This said, perhaps don't sell it till you've actually decided!

Questions to consider

What does your wedding ring symbolize to you?

Do people in particular contexts know you are/were married?

Are you happy to answer questions about the absence/presence of your wedding ring?

Wedding mementoes

These are possibly some of the most difficult items to place. Do you keep them? Bin them? Give them to your ex to deal with?

The photos, place cards, trinkets, champagne corks… they all need to be homed somewhere – even if that is in your recycling bin. Yet these aren't just things, they're memories. They are a complex combination of happiness, sadness, and disappointment; fulfilled and unfulfilled dreams.

To keep them could feel like holding on to the marriage and something that no longer exists; yet the wedding is also a fact from the past and happened. However unhappy you are now, your wedding was hopefully a happy day at the time, and can be recognized as such. You may choose to hold on to them for your children, or just to retain one or two photographs or objects.

By the same token, getting rid of everything may feel liberating – but it may also feel like you are unintentionally erasing a large part of your life. While memories do exist in tangible objects, they also exist in the minds and hearts of people, and therefore throwing away photographs does not mean the day did not happen, but rather that you aren't ever needing to retain photographic proof that it did.

Whether you decide to sell your wedding outfit, bin the photos, or pack everything into boxes to decide upon at a later date, it needs to be a decision you will be happy with in the future. There is no sense of immediacy. Keeping things "in case" or until you feel better equipped to make a decision is sensible. I packed many objects up and sent them to my parents' house, as I couldn't decide what to do with them. As I write this, they are still there and I should probably dispose of them in some way at last!

If you decide to send the items to your spouse, consider your motives for doing this. Are you hoping they will feel guilty and return to you? Is it so that you do not have to make a difficult decision about what to do with them? These do not preclude you from giving the memories to your ex, but may help you make a clear and constructive decision on what to do with them.

Questions to consider

Do you want to keep wedding items for posterity?

Will you keep or give away the memories?

Will they be kept for any future children?

How do you feel about throwing them or giving them away? If you are unsure, a decision does not have to be taken now.

What did you do with your wedding mementoes?

Carol: Put them in a box and it is now in the loft; the wedding albums are on my bookshelf – I look at it all occasionally.

Rowena: Threw them away!

Decobe: Basically, I walked away from the lot, including wedding photos and even the wedding gift my best man had given us.

May: We have both kept some wedding photos. They are hidden away somewhere.

Decobe's story

I am now a seventy-two-year-old male divorcee of twenty-three years, having divorced after nearly twenty-three years of marriage. Married life produced two fantastic children. My daughter is now married to a church pastor and has given me three wonderful grandchildren. My son is a quadriplegic (from birth), who now lives in a residential care home.

My life plans went out of the window with the divorce, and I found it very difficult to adjust. Suicidal thoughts kept cropping up in my head, and on one occasion it nearly came to pass. However, it was never going to happen. God made sure of that.

Initially after the divorce I believed that my wife was a hundred per cent to blame for the break-up of the marriage after her affair and eventual marriage to the new man in her life. But as the saying goes, it takes two to tango. There were areas in our marriage that I could or should have sorted out, rather than letting them ride and hoping for the best. It's interesting how one sees things differently in retrospect.

Now I am living a contented and happy life on my own. I go to a lively church where I am accepted for who I am, and where I can be me, but at the same time I try to do what I believe God has called me to do.

Will I marry again? Probably not. I haven't been turned off the state of marriage, and I fervently believe in the privilege and sanctity of marriage. If the right lady came along I wouldn't resist, but I'm not actively seeking a new spouse, nor would I ever just live with a partner.

Chapter Eleven

What to Do about the Practicalities of Separation

Separating belongings

A good consideration at all points throughout the separation process is whether you will be happy with your behaviour in the future. Regret is a fairly thankless emotion, and while there may be regrets from your marriage, your actions now are ones that in the future you want to feel confident were at least fair. In the separation of possessions and "all our worldly goods" it is easy to stumble into feelings of entitlement: what is "mine" and what is "owed" because of the end of the marriage. When we entered into marriage, we chose to share everything, yet now the time has come to divide it all. Considering the longer-term implications of our decisions now will hopefully result in less future heartache.

To illustrate this, one of my biggest, and unexpected, stumbling blocks was our DVD collection. It wasn't so much the DVDs themselves, but what they had come to symbolize. When we'd begun dating, we never bought the same DVD, preferring to share them between us. So, on separation, we had to pull apart this joint collection, ten years in the making. And I was doing the sorting.

There were some fairly easy decisions to start with. Films I didn't like went in his pile. Others that I knew were "his" more than "mine" went there too. Films I liked more than he did went into my pile. Birthday and Christmas gifts were appropriately apportioned. And finally I was left with a large mutual selection. One of my key decision-making questions was from my friend Emily: if I got the film out to watch it, would I feel it was his? If the answer was yes, then I should give it away. I could, she reminded me, always buy another copy. When separating all the possessions, this is a good question to ask yourself. In keeping an item, will you feel it is truly "theirs" and you have somehow stolen it? Will you be able to replace it relatively easily?

Depending on how recently you married, some wedding presents may also feel more or less connected to one of you. If your wedding was relatively recent, or if items hold a familial tie, it may be appropriate to divide them according to the original relationship with the owner. Some possessions are always looked at as wedding gifts: you may wish to give them away to a new home if neither of you wants that reminder. However, other items will have long since lost any connection and are kept because of their usefulness or beauty. Whether you want to keep or be rid of an item is an entirely personal choice. I still have items in my possession that I am aware were wedding presents. If I get married again, I may choose to replace them, purely as they are from my first marriage – yet for now, the fact that they were a wedding gift never concerns me, and I love the items, so I've kept them!

A further question is how you will divide the items and whether you will do so together or individually. As my ex-husband had decided to leave and had, at the stage of officially divorcing, been living outside our marital home for fourteen months, he offered to let me continue living in what was our home, and I offered to buy him out. As I mentioned previously, one of my stipulations was that I be the one who packed up his things. I didn't want to get divorced. But this was what was happening. In our situation, this worked OK. It may be that it would be more appropriate to get a mediator, either a professional one or a friend, and to go through the house and work out what will belong to whom. If possible, it is useful to discuss with your ex what will work best. You may choose not to reveal your plan to be considerate and fair, but instead show that through your actions, speech, and demeanour. Keeping a calm and level head may also help to make the process less painful and tense for you.

Questions to consider

Is there anything that makes you concerned or anxious about the separation of your belongings? Write it down and try to consider why that is.

Is there a strategy to avoid that situation, or to temper it somehow (for example, the presence of a friend, or being away)?

How will you divide possessions: separately or together? Will there be space for discussion?

Will you need help in discussing this? Consider a mutual third party's presence in making these decisions if your divorce is not friendly.

In separating items, will you feel an item is "theirs" if you keep it?

Can the item be easily replaced by one of you?

Are there certain things you want to keep in order to deliberately cause hurt?

Are there items you would be particularly upset not to keep?

Are certain objects more appropriate for one of you to keep? If this will be contentious, try to discuss

*the reasons and consider whether you could jointly
purchase another so as to have "one each"?*

Objects of financial value

In separating your possessions there are also likely to be objects of
value, including property, vehicles, antiques, and larger items such
as furniture. The only objects that we owned of any great financial
value were the car and the home itself. Because we agreed that I
would buy him out of the home, were still on speaking terms, and I
was fortunate enough to have finance at my disposal, we chose to do
this outside of court proceedings, but kept a written record via email
of our mutually agreed decision in case of future disagreement.
This kept the proceedings simple, cheaper, and actually gave us
opportunities to be generous and considerate toward one another in
how we behaved. However, there may be a need for equity for one
or both spouses, meaning the house needs to be sold. While for one
of you this issue may be expedient and need completing as quickly
as possible, for the other it may be more important to achieve a high
price. It is good to be clear about what both your expectations are in
order to lessen frustrations in an already fraught time.

From a court perspective, it may also be necessary for the family
home to be retained in order to raise the children. This is frustrating
for the spouse wishing to leave and to establish a separate life, yet
may also frustrate the spouse remaining: they might feel tied into
an arrangement due to financial and familial necessity, when they
too would rather be released. Alternatively, it may feel beneficial to
them or to you. If the issue around finances becomes complex, it is
wise to seek professional support to ensure neither of you loses out,
or that neither will later bring the issue into proceedings in court.

In some instances, it may be necessary to give financial
recompense for the retaining of possessions. While we were
separated, we attempted to share the car. Due to my job being a

drive away, the main ownership of the car was mine. At times, my ex wanted to be able to travel further afield. In those times I felt trapped myself, as I no longer had the flexibility of travel at my disposal. For several reasons, including this, we decided to purchase a second car with some joint savings. At the time, a part of me felt aggrieved that he was the owner of the new car, while I got the older and less financially valuable one. Recalling why I wanted our original car helped me to let go of this emotion – I had not had to consider any potential problems with a new vehicle, or go to the inconvenience of searching for a car, which is why I had asked to keep the "old" one. When we began separating possessions, it was difficult not to choose to ask for recompense for my older vehicle, but the freedom of not needing to search, test, and buy a new car had been preferable: I had to simply let it go. It may be that joint finances are needed to invest in things in order to split the possessions fairly, or that one spouse will give a contribution to this. Keep a written record (perhaps on email), in order to have future evidence.

A further financial implication is that of pensions. This is a particularly important consideration if one of you has worked for a longer number of years while the other has either not worked or else has taken a part-time job in order to care for children from the marriage. As part of a divorce settlement, it is acceptable to ask about pensions: had the marriage not ended, this pension would have been shared. If you are being asked or required to share your pension or feel you are entitled to a share, it is good to consider the choice you, as a couple, made when deciding how to raise your family. Was your decision for one spouse not to work taken jointly? Did this decision have a time frame (for example, when our youngest child begins school, X will retrain/take a part-time job/go back to work)?

Questions to consider

Will there be an opportunity to request certain items?

Are there any items with familial ties?

Are there any objects of value that will need financial compensation?

If you are selling your home, what is your main goal? (Speed of sale, high price?)

What is your ex's main goal?

Will pensions be part of your financial settlement?

Will the financing of your divorce also be taken into account?

PART THREE
Moving On

Chapter Twelve

Emotions

Hope and disappointment

> *O Lord, all my longing is before you;*
> *my sighing is not hidden from you.*
> *My heart throbs; my strength fails me,*
> *And the light of my eyes – it has also gone*
> *from me.*
> **Psalm 38:9–10, ESV**

My emotion writes itself on my face. If you don't know me, you might think my eyes are usually dull and my face finds it hard to crack into a smile. If you know me, hiding the anguish in my eyes is hard; my face is taut, my posture clenched and ready to receive another blow.

The physical signs of relationship breakdown can be hard to hide. Our eyes may no longer be red from crying, but that's because there's been so many tears even the blood vessels have got used to it. The bags under our eyes have become permanent fixtures, because sleep feels impossible and we eventually drop into a deep sleep where our brain attempts to catch up with our emotions, leaving us just as tired on wake up. My shoulders became so tense that moving them was painful.

Questions to consider

How does your body hold or express tension?

Are there ways to alleviate this?

The physical repercussions of divorce and separation stressors are our body's way of telling us that something is not right. Of course, we know this, so resting and releasing the tension is important. Watch a sad film, snuggle up under a blanket and have a good cry – you can pretend it's just the film causing it. I used to go for a massage and have the tension physically worked out of my body. Go for a run or join a kickboxing class to release the anger and need to physically do something.

The writer of this poem, or psalm, poses two problems to God: I am crying out to you for what I want, and I am exhausted in trying to hope. Dealing with separation and divorce is exhausting, and rest is necessary. Hope is defined in the dictionary as a feeling of expectation or desire. We can try to control our desire, yet we continue to hope our marriage might be saved, our situation might change, or that we might escape without it being traumatic and drawn out.

Hoping against the odds

Separation, divorce, and relationship breakdown is a time when many questions are asked and when unknowns that we are hoping for and fearful of arise. In a place of marital breakdown, I found I could either turn to or away from God. The psalmist has turned to God: he has poured out all the longings, hopes and fears before him to the point of exhaustion and not knowing what to do any more.

As King Solomon, full of wisdom, stated: "Hope deferred makes the heart sick, but a longing fulfilled is the tree of life."[9]

9   Proverbs 13:12.

This is precisely what it feels like when what you hope for, and long for, and yearn deeply for does not come to fruition. When hope is extinguished, it is like the light going out of your soul. Your heart, evidence suggests, can actually break – perhaps not snapping in two as cartoons suggest but physically altering because of the emotional pain.

Maybe you've experienced a situation like this. If you recall the moment, you can probably remember the bile rising in your throat, the constriction of your chest, the bottom falling out of your world, and being unable to fully comprehend the way life will never be completely the same again.

Thousands of years before Solomon, Job, who had lost his entire family, all his wealth, and finally his health, cried a similar sentiment:

> *"If only my anguish could be weighed and all*
> *my misery be placed on the scales! It would*
> *surely outweigh the sand of the seas – no*
> *wonder my words have been impetuous...*
> *What strength do I have, that I should still*
> *hope? What prospects, that I should be*
> *patient?"*
> **Job 6:2–3, 11**

Why hope? *Why?* Everything had been extinguished and there was nothing left for Job to hold on to. In the scale of hanging on by the fingernails, he was free-falling while his nails had torn out of his fingers: there was nothing. He was exhausted and there were no prospects on the horizon. That heaviness of anguish and misery is not unknown to me, and perhaps not to you.

But regardless of circumstances, from deep inside, somewhere, Job was hoping. Hoping things would change, his health might improve, that God would take pity on him and end his suffering completely. To be human is to hope. It's why people fight against injustice, and continue in the face of unbelievable adversity. It's why in the midst of separation, we might hope our spouse's heart will soften and they will return. We hope their eyes will be opened. We hope we can begin afresh and work through the circumstances to become ourselves again.

But hope is hard. It grows out of a desire. You can be active in pursuing the goal, you can keep doors open and options on the table, pushing at different doors to see if they're open to you. Yet hope in this situation seems to stem from that inability to really do what it is you're wanting. You can't lay hold of what your heart desires; instead you hope.

It is exhausting and all-consuming. It is waiting and wondering. It is running towards a dream while a potential reality is chained to your wrist. I can recall the weight of it with me, for a year and a half. Hope, whether realistic or dreaming of the improbable, was my watchword. It was the centre of my thoughts, the barrier around my soul. It kept me together. The tiny flickers of hope about my marriage, my job, my future.

Because hope is that flicker, the keeping alive of dreams and the thought so sacred it can sometimes not even be uttered. To fully verbalize what I wanted to happen felt like sharing that birthday wish as you blow out the candles – if you say it out loud, it won't happen. It embodied my waking thoughts, my dreams, and all my subconscious ideas. Occasionally hope would be fulfilled and I would blossom like that tree of life. More often it would be crushed underfoot and my heart would be sickened once again.

Hope helped me continue when all seemed lost. Hope allowed me to dream and glimpse a light from beneath a canopy so dark it seemed impenetrable.

Questions to consider

What does the word hope make you feel?

What are your hopes for your marriage? Is hoping realistic?

There was a long time in my marriage when I didn't know if it would ever be reconciled. I didn't know if everything I'd ever wanted would be lost. Hope was all I had to cling to. It is sometimes the only thing that can keep you from falling into despair. It is that tiny flicker of light in an otherwise darkened room.

A couple of years ago, I stumbled across a blog by a pastor from a church I had attended some time before. His wife, an incredible woman, was dying. What humbled me most, and still moves and inspires me now, was their hope. I have no doubt they hoped she would be healed. But she also had an assurance, a hope, in where she was headed. An unshakable hope fixed in Jesus and knowing that she would be meeting Him at that pivotal moment. I hope I have that same assurance and hope when I am at that point too. What an incredible hope to have.

We don't very often associate death with hope. We don't associate hope with feeling powerless, and not being able to control where things are headed. But hope sets you free, even when your world is falling apart.

I identified with *Shawshank Redemption*'s Red, who had been imprisoned much of his life, yet ultimately had the hope that one day he might be released. A glimmer of hope kept me from drowning in sorrow and being overwhelmed by grief. I believed, like Red, that there had to be something, somewhere, that would break through the darkness. We need hope to sustain us. We need hope to keep us going through the toughest points. Yet sometimes that hope doesn't come from within; we need to be given hope by someone else.

Red's friend Andy did this for him, giving him glimmers of what could be, even in the midst of a situation he was locked into where he was at the mercy of others. Ultimately, in a potentially frightening unknown, this was what gave Red the hope and perseverance to keep going.

Questions to consider

What is the biggest fear that keeps you prisoner?

What is your hope in? Are there experiential hopes in your life that do not depend on others for fulfilment?

Having hope means having to accept the possibility of disappointment. The night before my interview for a job I had long wanted I read these Bible verses, and I was cross: "Such hope never disappoints us, because God's love has been abundantly poured out within our hearts through the Holy Spirit who was given to us."[10]

These verses in Romans shouldn't be read out of context. Hope might well disappoint me, ranted my interior monologue. Yet I had not read to the end of the sentence: it is hope *in Jesus* that does not disappoint us. Ultimately, my hope did disappoint me: I didn't get the job. My hopes for my marriage were ultimately disappointed. Disappointed hopes are one of life's most painful situations. So where do we find our hope? How do we manage hope when we're convinced we will be disappointed?

In the midst of my own darkest moments, I realized I couldn't keep myself going. Maintaining hope without help had become almost impossible. Others around me would help to keep a spark of hope alive, be that for my marriage or for me personally. I tried to

10 Romans 5:5, AMP.

focus on things I was looking forward to, even while I hoped for the reconciliation that never happened.

Questions to consider

How does the idea of hope make you feel in your situation?

Do you need help to continue to hope?

What are your hopes for you personally by the end of this stage in your life?

Are there any small ways you can find fulfilled hopes in your everyday life?

What or who gave you hope in the midst of divorce and despair?

Carol: My faith was the only thing that kept me going: knowing that things are part of a bigger plan. Though I was very angry with God for not stopping me from marrying in the first place; for not making any warning signs, if there were any, really clear to me. My small group from church were invaluable – they didn't judge and just accepted me as I was at any particular time. They were a great source of laughter, which was sorely needed and helped get me on the road to recovery.

Decobe: I suspect it was the few true friends I had left following the divorce. Also, I was clinging on to God for all I was worth, but deep down not really sure whether God would come through for me. He did, of course, but Satan had in those years just about totally convinced me that I was on my own.

Ellie: Although I have believed in God for as long as I can remember, nothing has ever made me question my faith as much as going through separation and divorce. The Bible says, "God is our refuge and strength, an ever-present help in trouble" (Psalm 46:1) and I found it proved true. When you get to the end of yourself, you realize that you really do need God. Numerous times I cried and prayed, saying exactly how I felt, without any pretence. While our marriage was not miraculously restored, over time I saw circumstances within the situation change, and also my attitude and thinking was affected, helping me to cope better. As the old hymn "Great is Thy Faithfulness" says, Jesus gives "Strength for today and bright hope for tomorrow".

May: I made goals sometimes: small short-term things I wanted to achieve to keep me going. Friends reassured me. I used to visit some friends of my parents occasionally and we would go for walks; they had geese and a dog that I enjoyed the company of too. These visits were refreshing, as was sailing with a bunch of friends I had been sailing with for ten years.

Rowena: I had no kind of faith to speak of at the time. I just got on with things, as these things happen. My friends were my biggest support network.

Disappointed dreams

Divorce is the destroyer of dreams. It is the developer of new dreams. As we negotiate separation and divorce, we begin to encounter and acknowledge the dreams particular to our individual selves, our marriage, and the dreams of those around us concerning our marriage. The realization and acceptance that these will not be fulfilled can be an extremely painful process that is sadly not limited in length. It is a period of mourning, involving similar stages to grief.

Unacknowledged and unaccepted, our dreams can become barriers to a fulfilling life post-divorce. We are wise to work through them as we encounter them, and also to face them as a painful reality: what these dreams meant to us and what they may mean for our future. We are released to dream anew – new avenues for our old dreams – and also in new directions.

How the verses at the start of this chapter resonated with me. My longing for my marriage to work was immense. My desire to be a mother had been with me since childhood. The light had indeed gone from my eyes. I was crushed. Some of these dreams we are being forced to lose will feel painfully obvious to us. Perhaps you wished to have children; perhaps to have your children grow up with both parents in a loving, committed relationship with one another. Perhaps it was to move to a particular location; to work in a particular field; to holiday in a certain place. Whatever the dream was, the reality is now disappointment.

Dreams within a marriage can take two people to fulfil them. In some circumstances, this can involve one partner being the advocate, support, or encourager, while the other is more active. In other circumstances, the two must work together in order to achieve the goal, although again this may look different in terms of action from one to the other.

But imagine turning around to your spouse and sharing a dream. "You'll never achieve that," they respond. Perhaps this has happened to you. Perhaps you were the one uttering the words. If you do not dream together, you may begin to dream alone. In healthy marriage, this may involve helping one partner to strategize or consider the steps to realistically achieving that dream. It may involve sacrifice, or careful consideration, and a gentle fanning of a flame for many years. But if the dream is quenched, there is the possibility of resentment, emotional detachment, and emotional attachment to those who are supportive of that dream.

As we approach divorce, it is worth considering whether we had, in fact, stopped talking about our dreams. It is easy to think we are discussing them, especially if they feature prominently in our own minds. All too often, we can be pursuing and moving towards a dream without discussing how our minds have changed, doubts that are emerging or fears we have about the change it may bring in our lives. There are many different dreams: family, home, church involvement, volunteering, work/career, where to spend our money, time spent together, holidays…

Questions to consider

Had you recently discussed your dreams? Consider the above categories and dreams you may have shared.

Had you discussed your doubts and desires in connection with these?

In your heart of hearts, what dreams did you hope your marriage would fulfil?

Which dreams are the most painful to consider living without?

Dreaming new dreams

There is a huge grief that follows the removal of the possibility of these dreams. The fact that they were not a reality, does not mean they should not be mourned. Part of a partnership is discussing what you are moving towards, working through difficulties together, and aiming towards that in whatever way best suits the two of you. This lack of partnership means that dreams may no longer be achievable, realistic, possible, or perhaps simply that they will take a different course.

Of course, this change of dream may not be as negative an experience as we may expect. During my separation I decided on a career change. The challenges I had experienced in my job (primary teaching) had continued – namely workload and pressure – and I decided, now I was no longer considering the possibility of maternity in the near future, I could not continue with the sixty-hour week and long holidays trade-off. Ironically, in marriage, I would have been unlikely to pursue this – the new job I embarked on was almost four hours of commuting each day, and I would have seen this as eating into our time together. Our separation meant I had only myself to focus on as regards career – discussion of our dreams had taken a sabbatical – and I looked further afield. By the time we decided to divorce, I was six months into a dream job, earning a fraction of what I'd earned before, but with new dreams on the horizon. There was the possibility of moving to the location of my new job. New location meant a new house, new church, new friends. The possibilities seemed endless. The destruction of my old dreams posed a new dream, and endless possibility.

The disappointed dreams gave space for new dreams to emerge and flourish. If you'd told me when I found out he was cheating the kind of dreams that would fill my mind two years on, I wouldn't have believed you. They would never have been dreams I'd expected to fulfil in my marriage, including becoming a published author. The death of dreams doesn't mean the death of all dreams. Sometimes, they happen in ways you least expect them to.

Questions to consider

Are there any dreams or ideas you have put off because of your marriage?

Post separation and divorce, did you fulfil an unexpected or previously unattainable dream?

Fear of the future

The contrast between hope and fear exists in a distinct way in relationships. For a relationship to work it requires vulnerability, which if you have been hurt is extremely difficult. Is it worth becoming vulnerable again in case you are further hurt? The fear of the same problem recurring is there, even while you hope the marriage will be mended. The oxymoron of a hope–fear desire for your marriage is a confusing one. In the midst of hoping my marriage would be restored, I was also fearful. There were so many questions in tandem with my hope that I could hardly bear to ask. For me these questions predominantly related to trust. How could trust be re-established? Would I ever be able to trust him fully again? What about issues we already found challenging in our marriage – would we be able to resolve them now? In every thought and desire for our marriage to work out and for us to remain together, I had a niggling doubt at the back of my mind: I just didn't know how things would pan out if we did stay together, and that was frightening. It was frightening particularly as the staying together was what I was striving for yet the thought of it was almost as terrifying as breaking up.

Perhaps you have other fears. Is their commitment, or your own, simply going to fade out again? Will a particular issue rear its head again?

The overwhelming desire for your marriage to work becomes intrinsically linked with fears about the future of your marriage if things do work out and it can be hard to establish which one you are really hoping for. The fears can make it feel that an end and resolution would be preferable, a relief that you don't need to deal with the problems in this format any longer. In some instances this is positive. If you are experiencing any form of abuse – physical or emotional – then the fear is a necessary and positive emotion to help remove you from the situation. It can also help you see the positives when the relationship does end. Yes, there may be complex things to deal with, but there will also be some fears that are not now everyday, lifelong realities.

A strategy I found incredibly helpful was to mind-map my life. You may prefer lists, subheadings, underlining, colour-coding, or sticky notes – however your mind best works! But the aim of the process is to consider all the key areas of your life. Think about your relationship, friendships, family, work, hobbies – every conceivable area. For each, begin to list the hopes and the fears, the positives and negatives for each area. I began using two colours. I listed the dreams I (we'd) had, the emotions, questions, concerns, positive turns, everything that came to mind as I sat and thought. I thought about tomorrow and also far into the future. Acknowledging them was hard but having them clearly written down allowed me to see where my major concerns lay: the first was with trust, the second was his commitment to our marriage, and the third was my work, where I felt overwhelmed in an already overwhelming time.

Being honest about my fears also allowed me to feel a sense of relief when he decided to divorce. While I did not want a divorce and wanted to remain married, I was able to acknowledge how awful things had been since the problems began and was able to express relief that I would not need to negotiate the "trust" question with him. I knew I would need to explore it, but rather in the context of how I would and could trust in the future, rather than trying to trust someone who had repeatedly lied to me.

Speaking the fears out, or writing them down, also prevents them from having control over our minds. Living in fear or with fear is not a healthy or helpful place long term. While it can be necessary in the short term – adrenaline has its place in the body for a reason – it is not a long-term positive in a relationship.

Questions to consider

What do you hope will happen in your marriage? Write down your hopes, no matter how unrealistic you think they are.

What are your fears? Why are you afraid of these things happening?

What was your biggest fear in separating and divorcing?

Carol: I'm not sure I was afraid. My biggest emotion was relief I think because the twelve years of my marriage had been awful. I was embarrassed and anxious about telling my parents. I didn't really want to have to tell them the reasons. I was looking forward to getting a life back and not being so isolated.

Decobe: Probably the biggest fear in separating and divorcing for me was creating a new person in myself. I had, during the married years, become somebody else, not really me. Now, with the bleak outlook that I was faced with, whether I could, or even wanted to, be the real me again was something I dreaded.

Ellie: I remember a whole host of questions coming to mind after our initial conversation when I found out something big was wrong. It must have been due to shock. What would I do if he left for good? Would I still continue in my job? Would I change my name? All sorts of questions which weren't necessary to be concerned with at the time. It turned out to be sufficiently challenging just to make it through each day! I did eventually face these questions and many others in time when I needed to, a lot later on. I wouldn't say I feared being on my own, as I've always been quite independent, but I did fear the possibility of him not being part of my life for ever. I dreaded the thought of not seeing him again. It seemed so final, not unlike when someone dies.

May: The fear in divorcing was that I would not be able to afford to live in a safe area in a house I liked; it would be a change in standards of living. I would feel lonely as well, living in a different area from my friends.

Rowena: I'm not really sure I had one. By the time we actually separated away from each other and I moved back to the UK I had moved on emotionally and was ready to enjoy life. I think I did all my grieving earlier on in the process.

Abandonment, inadequacy, and self-esteem

These are the emotions that for me personally most symbolized my separation. As my friend Ellie wisely said, your spouse isn't dead, which is good (despite how you may be feeling), but in some ways the fact they chose to leave makes it harder. In death someone has no option, and their love still exists for you; it never diminished. In separation and divorce that love has deliberately been removed and perhaps redirected elsewhere. In speaking to a friend who had experienced the death of her first spouse and divorce with her second, she said they felt broadly similar – but people knew less what to say to her about the divorce.

Regarding my own particular situation I felt that I must somehow have been lacking. I wasn't sure how or in what way, but my self-esteem hit an all-time low. I felt I was not, and had not been, enough. Not pretty enough. Not sexy enough. Not listening enough. Not communicating enough. Not home enough, not submissive enough, just never ever enough.

Being "enough" became a by-word for whether I felt I was adequate for a situation. Was I beautiful enough? Was I intelligent enough? Was I good enough?

It wasn't until I began writing this book that I realized I had felt this way. Being enough had become intrinsically tied to what I would think. Each day it might manifest itself differently. Some days I did feel enough, but often in some small way, I would not.

My worth in being enough had become dependent on one instance in my life. My mind did not focus on the many times I had been more than enough; when I had been wonderful and fulfilling, more than simply enough; it traversed back to that one time I perceived that I was not. Thinking that I should somehow have been "more" and "enough" also suggested to me that I needed to be perfect, even while understanding that no one is. The idea that I should have "been enough" did not allow for someone else's actions or responses or choices. I could have been perfect and it would not have precluded the opportunity for someone else to not choose to commit to me. This is hard and painful, tying in as it does to a feeling of rejection. Nothing I could have done would have been enough.

In exploring this further with a counsellor, she flipped the question around. "What," she said, "if you asked whether he was enough? Was he committed enough? Communicating enough?" All the enoughs… Neither of us was perfect, but the idea that the burden of "enoughness" didn't simply lie with me was a revelation. It wasn't my inadequacy that had caused this to happen. She also asked me, what the definition of "enough" was. I had no answer. Somehow in my head I needed to be "enough" yet didn't have a barometer of what this was or what it looked like. Releasing myself from the mythical need to be enough is a constant battle, yet a liberating one to fight.

In the Bible, in chapter 31 of Proverbs, there is a description of a great woman. One phrase is about her external appearance, and over twenty phrases describe her character. This is the element we have control over; my character was something I could allow to be refined and honed through separation and divorce, or hardened. I could work on becoming a person I wanted to be, or allow myself to evolve into someone I didn't recognize, know, or like.

However, not feeling "enough" hasn't stopped with finding out who I am. I have become slightly less apologetic for who I am, and have been able to remember that while no one person has been "enough" in supporting me in divorce and separation because simply no one person can be, I equally do not have to and cannot fulfil this role in someone else's life.

Questions to consider

Which emotions do you battle with since your separation?

Are there particular causes or triggers for these emotions?

Can you, as my counsellor did, flip these on their head and ask the opposing question?

Regret

Regret can very quickly be tied in with blaming oneself for decisions and thinking that if only we'd done things differently it would've worked out better. To begin with, it is important to acknowledge the good. It is usually past tense but regretting the future combines the sadness and disappointment of things that have not come to pass and dreams that will now not be realities. Regret also encompasses that feeling of wishing you had done things differently, the "what if?" and the possible consequences. It can be a helpful emotion, but is not a healthy place to remain.

When I got married I was on the cusp of taking my first teaching role. As I referred to earlier, teaching is an all-consuming job, and while I tried not to let it consume my life, there were many evenings and weekends spent working. There were times when I did not come home from work as early as I would have wanted to, or contribute as much to the running of the household as I would have liked.

Did I regret this? I certainly wished I had come home earlier, and invested the time into my marriage relationship instead of my work. I also know how hard I worked, how I still didn't do all I could in teaching and how ultimately I chose to give up that particular career because of the pressure on the rest of my life. I know that it brought in a wage we needed and so that was good for our marriage.

This is one small example of an element I regretted, because I wished I had chosen differently. It had an impact on our marriage, whether we communicated about it well or not – and sometimes we did, other times we didn't. Would we still be divorced if I had done something differently? I don't know. I can't know. Whether living differently would have changed our relationship I couldn't say, so I have to leave that regret in the past. There may be instances that you feel changed the course of your marriage irrevocably that were your actions or those of your spouse; while these are past actions, there may be present possibilities or positive choices you can make to rectify them.

One question I have been asked, in various forms, since my marriage ended, was whether I had any regrets surrounding my marriage. Did I regret getting married? Did I regret not having children?

To all of these, my answer was the same. It did happen. And we didn't have children.

It is in the past. I cannot change the past.

These two statements are freeing. You cannot change the past. You cannot change the choices you made in your marriage, outside of it, or any actions you took.

Where regret is helpful is in repentance. When regret equals repentance, we have the opportunity to change. Repentance is not simply saying "sorry"; it is choosing to live differently in the future.

It is worth taking time to consider whether you have committed actions that need repenting of. Perhaps you have the opportunity to apologize for your actions? This might not be appropriate in your circumstances. But regret is an emotion that needs to pass eventually.

Questions to consider

What do you wish you had done differently?

How can you forgive yourself for the choices you made then?

Regret is damaging to us because it involves looking back and wishing. None of us can change the past. As we move forward, a great question to ask ourselves as we approach decision-making is "Do I feel I will regret this decision?" If you feel you might, take time to reconsider and perhaps make a different choice. When looking back afterwards, hopefully you will feel you made the decision with the best of intentions and hopes at the time.

Chapter Thirteen

Combining Past and Present

A new normal

Have you ever seen a toddler collecting toys? They mill about the room picking up toys until their arms are completely full. Yet they don't stop – they continue attempting to pick up new toys, dropping others in the process. And we can be much like this toddler in our lives. We hold on to dreams, ideals, and plans, yet sometimes it is necessary for us to lay some of these down in order to take hold of what is next.

Whatever plans we had together with our ex-spouse, they may now not go ahead, or else may be fulfilled without our partner. This doesn't mean there is nothing yet to come, but it does mean we will need to grieve those experiences we have not had, in order to fully embrace the newer ones.

As the period of separation lengthens and the divorce process completes, our options are to hold on to the old dreams, ways, and ideas, or to drop them and pick up new ones. Flinging everything down at once and turning things on their head isn't necessarily the answer! For some people a wholesale change might help. For others, it's the stuff of nightmares. You might also find you're not on the same side of the fence you would ordinarily be on. To begin with, we must start to embrace our "new normal". The "new normal" is the abnormal or the change that we begin to see as usual life. Instead of thinking of it as the different way, we begin to see it as the ordinary way of things. This is often just the small things. Perhaps it's being comfortable going to bed alone, even enjoying the space available. That moment you define yourself without hesitation or without stumbling over being single. When you make plans and don't consider your ex-spouse's social calendar, availability, or opinion.

There may be many things you are finding a challenge in your new normality. Perhaps make a list of them to return to in a few weeks' or months' time. Has your opinion on them changed? Do they bother you in quite the same way as they did before? Allowing our new normal to become just that is a gradual process with the understandable celebrations and setbacks of any life-changing event along the way. So remember to celebrate when you hope, look forward, and are happy, congratulating yourself for your steps going forward. You are not simply the sum of your past: you will have new hopes and dreams where you have had disappointment, and that, in itself, gives us a glimmer of hope.

Questions to consider

What dreams, ideas, and lifestyles are you holding on to from the past?

Is there an aspect of your new normality you quite like, or even enjoy? Make a list of all the things you feel have changed positively.

What would be one thing you would like to feel is "normal" to you? Revisit this in a few weeks' or months' time.

Was there a long-held dream that came to fruition partly because of your separation and divorce?

Rowena: Not really. My marriage hadn't been awful. It was a shock that it ended, but I didn't really think in terms of "life goals I wanted to achieve". I wasn't thinking long-term – just in getting through, day by day.

Carol: I went to Norway to see the Northern Lights. I was there for a week and had a great adventure.

Decobe: I knew I had become a different person during the married years, but I always longed to be the real me. Surprisingly, to me at least, this actually materialized over the years following divorce, and I can now honestly be me again.

Ellie: Life is certainly an adventure, and at times a rollercoaster! While the lowest point so far for me has definitely been separation and divorce, the journey I have been on since has contained some incredible highs. This has included obtaining a significant promotion at work, moving abroad to volunteer in a developing country for over two years, and coming back to the UK to navigate a new career path which more closely aligns to my passions and values. I wouldn't give the credit for any of this to divorce! But when life falls apart it forces you to examine who you really are and how you want to live. I have been surrounded by wonderful friends and family who have helped me to be courageous in pursuing new opportunities and long-held dreams. I now live in a different city and have made a new life, but without running away from my experiences and while still valuing what was.

May: The dream was to be able to be myself and happy again. And to not have to do loads of paperwork for the divorce all the time!

Talking about the past

The reason we are sad at the loss of our marriage or relationship is because there were probably, at one time, good, positive elements there. We are sad at the loss of opportunities and a joint future or have regret over decisions we have made. We may feel we have made the right decision to separate, divorce, or move on, but we can still feel sad; the two are not mutually exclusive.

Remembering the positives, while painful, enables us to remember our marriage was (if only at times) worthwhile, healthy, and an investment we fully believed in. Any attempt to diminish this could make us feel the marriage was a waste of time, when in fact, it was an investment made in good faith; the fact the return was not as expected, does not mean the choice to invest was necessarily foolish.

Recalling happy times also gives us a sort of "permission" to see anniversaries differently. We may well wish things were different and spend whole days crying – we are after all mourning a loss and grieving for our marriage and circumstances. Much as a funeral is a complex combination of what was good and positive in someone's life combined with sadness at their passing, so no-longer-anniversaries can provide that same complexity and challenge.

Talking about our past can be difficult to negotiate as we transition into a new phase of our lives, particularly as people know less about our situation as it becomes less immediate.

Question to consider

Can you recall or list some happy moments from your marriage when the two of you enjoyed yourselves together?

Knowledge that's not my skill set

Speaking about life becomes difficult when you are in an environment where you have a great deal of knowledge and very little skill. Familiarity with technical language and a vast comprehension of how something works without actually being able to do it yourself is hard to conceal. Through my ex's hobby, I knew a surprising amount about guitars for someone who has never played, and only picked one up to dust it. However, if I entered into a discussion or admitted some prior knowledge, the conversation could then lead down a path of explaining why and how I knew so much yet couldn't play a note. And it's for this reason it's sometimes easier post-separation to pretend swathes of your knowledge don't exist.

Deciding whether to get involved in a conversation may depend on how essential the information is – if it's going to win your team the pub quiz, get involved! By considering how you might explain your familiarity if asked, you may find it easier to decide about whether you speak up. If a casual "Oh, my ex had a motorbike" suffices without vast explanation it may feel simpler to speak up than if it requires a relationship history explanation of the hobbies of your ex-spouse and the fact you were married.

Gradually, your knowledge may decrease or dim as it becomes less relevant to daily life and therefore the pressure or desire to get involved in a conversation can diminish too. My knowledge about guitars is now sketchier, although I would now have fewer qualms about throwing in a comment about my ex having had several. Speaking more freely also links to whether people are aware of your past and therefore your ex's skill set; if they are not, it once again leads to the decision as to whether to drop them into conversation, or to avoid the conversation and potentially their existence altogether.

This can be a further loss to experience. Our familiarity with and presence in that arena is curtailed. Now this may be met with much joy: maybe you hated their hobby, or disliked joining in, or felt it ate into your time together. But maybe you enjoyed knowing about that particular area and having a deep knowledge that you didn't have to practise as a hobby yourself. There is nothing to prevent you from taking up the hobby as your own if you wish. It's not copying your ex, but a decision that you enjoyed that particular hobby and will therefore continue to do it independently, not letting the fact they have that same hobby stop you.

Questions to consider

Do you feel you have knowledge which is not your skill set?

Are you proud of that knowledge?

How do you feel about its loss and the loss of involvement in that sphere?

Would you want to explain the context of your knowledge? You may feel differently according to environments and situations.

Talking about your marriage

Conversations about weddings and marriage can be tricky to navigate when your own has broken down. When the topic comes around, jumping in with "On my wedding day", "When I was planning my wedding", or "Yes, when I was married" feels slightly odd. The trouble is, my marriage broke down and ended. They are describing a happy occasion and although my wedding day was joyous, the marriage ultimately wasn't. It becomes hard to feel that any of your wedding and marriage advice or stories have value. Yet simply because our marriages have ended does not make our experience invalid or of less value. If anything, we may also have insight that others do not; perhaps the benefit of hindsight helps us out, or simply our experiences bring a different slant on an old problem.

For those separated and divorced, it's surprisingly affirming when someone acknowledges your wedding and experiences, regardless of outcome. It feels like they too know there were happier times, and do not disregard the value of your life experiences. Their casual mention of it affirms their knowledge of you and the way you are comfortable enough with each other, to discuss even the bad bits. Later when I was single and thinking about dating, a person's reaction to my previous marriage would sway me quickly toward or away from them: I wanted someone to be fine with it, and even bandy it around in conversation when appropriate!

But eventually, I talked about my wedding when others talked about theirs. A group of us (one married, one engaged, one in a relationship, and me) were chatting over the impending nuptials and whether you cried or would cry at your own wedding. My friends know me well, and I could talk freely. What I hadn't been prepared for was the feeling as I recalled that moment when the doors opened for me to walk down the aisle. It was a moment of intense emotion in my life, and not one I'd thought of since I'd separated. I didn't want it back, but I hadn't appreciated that one day I would dig it up and think it over again now I was divorced. That's one of the funny things about divorce, occasionally, when you think it's all dealt with and just an increasingly distant memory, it socks you one, just to remind you it's still there.

Being aware that talking about your wedding and marriage may bring up long-forgotten emotions means it may help to drop the occasional off-the-cuff comment into conversation before having longer conversations, or that perhaps you would want to be in a "safe" space with people who know you well in case you do get upset. I had never thought I would look back on that moment with anything other than joy, and it was a hard memory to recollect. Spending time thinking over the day may help you to grieve it too. After that initial gut-wrench and ensuing emotion to sort through, no longer did that memory hold any emotion for me, and it was something I could discuss in a detached way. You may find you never detach from the emotion and memory; neither is the "correct" way to process.

The amount you talk about marriage or the wedding is entirely up to you, much as the amount you may or may not wish to talk about the separation and divorce. Your wedding and marriage still have value in the learning of lessons, the sharing of experience, and in our lives too. Even as you move on from your marriage, your future is shaped and altered because of it. This doesn't have to be a negative thing. Far from it, we may find much happiness, fulfilment, and new parts of ourselves we hitherto didn't know existed. But we are shaped because of our marriages; therefore they – our memories and our experiences – have value that can be shared.

Questions to consider

Are there particular lessons you feel you learned from your marriage?

How was your wedding day? Which thoughts resonate as you think back over it?

How do you feel at the prospect of talking about your marriage?

How much do I tell new friends?

One great freedom in divorce is making new friends, but one point to decide on is whether to be upfront when meeting new people. The closer to the instance of separation and divorce you are, the more likely you are to be upfront. It is the most preoccupying part of your life, and it may come out more quickly. Alternatively, it may be the part of your life you most wish to conceal. Eventually though, pretending one key experience of your life does not exist becomes impossible. It did happen, so being upfront becomes necessary and inevitable, although simultaneously less all consuming.

Waiting for conversational circumstance to allow for a natural mention of your previous marriage is one way to be upfront and honest. As it is absorbed into the conversation, it may pass by seemingly unnoticed but as a drop of information for others. Questions could follow, yet the natural flow of conversation allows you to be upfront at whatever level you might wish.

Being upfront about what's happening in your life is incredibly difficult, especially when it feels raw. At what point do you casually drop into conversation that you're divorced? The potential of being faced with someone's head slightly to the left or right, with a sympathetic gaze and an earnestly meant "I'm sorry" might feel totally at odds with where you're at. Or, as from my personal experience, there can be stunned silence following the announcement, in which the fellow conversationalist is at a loss for what to say next. Sometimes, to avoid putting other people in awkward positions we simply suppress this part of our life. It's easier to keep it concealed than to feel the need to apologize for creating awkwardness via your atypical life path, or to reassure someone you're not really that bothered, as it was a very long time ago. ("No, honestly, I really am fine with it.")

The boldness and honesty required to even face the fact separation has happened takes time itself. So cut yourself some slack if you can't be upfront straight away; it's not only justifiable, it's completely normal. For some friendships or passing relationships, it may never come up. The moment to be subtly upfront never arrives and so they never know this part of your past. And that's perfectly acceptable too. There are many things we don't mention about our lives, and just because it took up a few years doesn't mean we *have* to talk about it. After all, my school qualifications and degree took up years of my life, yet rarely crop up in conversation, and my former marriage doesn't need to either.

Chapter Fourteen

When Other People's Lives Move On

My life is going backwards

My best description of what life equated to post-marital split was that someone had rewound a video of my life twelve years to the last time I was single and announced that I was going to need to start again – albeit twelve years older than I was at the start. My separation happened in my mid-twenties. In some senses, that is an ideal time; once your marriage is dissolved, you still have time to rediscover yourself, your career, and even to embark on another relationship and possible future family. In other senses it's less than ideal because around you seemingly *everyone* you know is doing what you were doing mere months ago. There's engagement announcements, weddings, and baby scan photos all over your social media accounts, and even if you manage to avoid those, your closest friends are experiencing hopeful, exciting, life-changing moments around you. I wasn't sure whether I felt my marriage had been a waste of time – I was by no means as young as I was. Becoming suddenly separated and single placed me somehow back at the start point of a race I felt I'd been running just fine. I was there alone, disadvantaged by the many runners now somehow vastly ahead of me – at least in terms of self-awareness if not relationship status.

Looked at realistically, this was of course not actually true. By no means was I the only one single, unmarried, or without children. I was not the only one whose life had not mapped out as they expected. I was, sadly, one of a number of Christian couples I knew and had heard about, in their twenties, getting divorced. But to my skewed perspective, everyone else seemed to be heading off into the sunshine of their dreams, marriage on the horizon, baby in tow, or investing in a long-term future. Those who were single and had maybe dreamed of being married seemed confident in who they were and were processing their futures light years ahead of me. My future went about as far as next week, and at many stages not even as far as that.

Celebrating with others

While all can seem brilliant and an experience of dreams fulfilled, we can never know the inside of anyone else's life. Although to us as outsiders, all can seem rosy, this may not actually be the case. Everyone's life holds stories of, if not life going backwards, at least going on a detour to the original destination, or changing destination altogether. Instinctively we tend to hold those things inside, and don't speak about them except to those closest to us. It's easier to be considerate when you know, but these things are hard to share. Just as many people may not see the hopes, current or broken, in our heart, we also do not see the challenges others are facing. When you're divorcing or separated, watching people get married, have babies, and simply rejoice in new life experiences is really tough. It's the combination of complete joy in seeing people celebrate great and momentous times in their lives, coupled with the immeasurable pain of losing something incredibly precious, something you no longer have, and dreams crushed and unfulfilled. It felt like everyone was getting married and having babies except me – I was doing the opposite: I was getting divorced. Everyone else's dreams seemed to be coming to fruition, except for mine.

When we hear announcements like these, it simply pierces our heart a little more. How do we live with this tension – this juxtaposition of our deep-rooted desire with our delight for our friends? As a wise friend said to me, you have to enjoy the moment and then be sad later. This isn't easy. To paraphrase Coldplay – I hadn't expected it to be easy, but also hadn't expected it to be quite so hard. But whenever I've tried to put the advice of my friend into practice, I've ended up enjoying weddings and new baby announcements far more than I'd ever anticipated. That said, as I'll explore later, I've then gone home devastated for myself.

In the middle of my separation, a couple we were extremely close to announced their second pregnancy. Some of my closest friends, single for many years, found new partners and began to set up home. I was a bridesmaid, not once but twice, before my divorce was finalized. I became an aunt. Meeting my nephew was one of the most elating experiences of my life, but I'd be lying if I didn't say how complex was the joy and pain of hearing that announcement, followed by the eight-month wait for the birth.

In the circumstances of experiencing other people's joyous moments that are exactly what you dreamed of for yourself, it's important to be honest. Have people who know you at the end of the phone. When we are divorcing, people can feel they shouldn't share their good news with us. But it doesn't mean we don't want to hear good news – we do! Hearing people's joyful news without giving any impression we resent it is a character strength. By letting people know how utterly delighted we are for them, and expressing our sadness with another friend, we can experience both sides of the emotive coin honestly. We will be genuinely pleased to share in their joy. And yes, at the same time, we can be sad for ourselves and grieve what life hasn't given us.

Watching other people live the life you had or want is tough. But survival is possible and sharing in their joy can actually make you the happiest you've felt in a long time.

The tension between celebration and self-preservation is a hard one to get right. There's no rule book, so if you were hoping for a "don't attend any events for the next six months" instruction, you're about to be disappointed. Only you can know what you can stand to celebrate and what might make you burst into tears. Be prepared to be surprised at your own resilience, and at your capacity for joy in the midst of your own disappointment and destroyed dreams. In fact, I would encourage you to challenge yourself to enter into situations that you think you might find hard and give yourself permission to leave early if you need to. At each juncture, what helped me was to acknowledge what I found hard about the situation and consider what I thought I might find hard beforehand.

Questions to consider

Which events or life experiences cause you most concern?

What about them do you think you will find hard?

What, if anything, are you glad about for the people or person involved?

Have those involved experienced anything of their own difficulties in reaching this point? Try to be thankful for the joy they are experiencing.

Can you share the joy you are experiencing with your friends, even while you feel sad yourself? Consider whether this might be easier to express in written form.

Around the time of separation or divorce, what was your experience of other people getting married/having children/retiring/experiencing life experiences you'd expected

Carol: I'm not sure I really noticed!

Decobe: I was actually thrilled when others were getting married or having children or any of the other things that people rather expected out of their lives. I know that it isn't related to this question, but I got very upset when facing others who were talking about divorcing; most of them seemed to treat it so lightly and felt marriage could easily be discarded if things didn't work out as they wanted. I still feel very strongly about this to this very day.

Ellie: At the beginning I was numb in my own grief but also very grateful for good friends, so could celebrate with them in their good news. At times I grew a little tired of engagement or baby news from other people because life seemed very routine and predictable for them when I had experienced that it wasn't so predictable for me. However, the Bible tells us to rejoice with those who rejoice and to mourn with those who mourn. I think that's the best way to be – we need each other in the highs and the lows. I found my experience gave me a much greater empathy for those enduring their own struggles and that people opened up to me much more easily. It's true that although we admire people for their strengths, we connect with them in our weaknesses.

May: Some people got divorced a lot quicker than we did; it made their situation look easy compared to ours. I preferred to go out and do activities rather than sit around with new babies. I did spend time playing musical instruments, sometimes with my friends' grandchildren and singing with them or walking or cycling. I married late so although we had tried to have children, we hadn't. Then, after the head injury happened, I was glad there were no children living with us that had to cope with his changed personality. He had step children – young adults who lived with his previous ex-wife – and they came to visit him less and less.

Rowena: I don't think it bothered me. I never wanted children at that time, so people having them was not something that upset me. In fact, I was glad I didn't have them after the way things turned out.

Engagements and weddings

While engagements can be held at more of a distance, weddings are all-day events. It's good to be realistic around them. The fact that you are separated or divorcing is testament to your own wedding, and however joyful or awful your own wedding, however devastated or relieved you are that it is over, it is likely that attending a wedding will bring emotions and memories to the fore.

Being part of a wedding gives me hope that one day, maybe, that could happen for me again. Love exists! It's possible for people to love one another for who they are. I remind myself I was loved like that; that I loved like that. It was true, whatever it feels like some days now. And I am deserving of love like that. You are deserving of love like that. We don't deserve it because of anything we have done, but because loving someone in that way is what marriage is about.

As you approach going to a wedding, it's important to be honest with both others and yourself. If you are close to the bride and groom, it may be helpful to speak about their wedding beforehand. Share how happy you are for them! Finding joy in another's happiness is helpful. It may not mean you are happy personally but that you are happy for them and therefore able to smile and rejoice. Presumably you have been invited because they would like you to share their day. If you are able to, perhaps ask which songs and readings they hope to have at their wedding and which pieces of entry and exit music. While you must keep these to yourself in the run-up so as not to spoil the surprise, you will also give yourself time to work through any emotions that may be brought up through any similarities to your own wedding. If it is being held in the same venue as yours, perhaps pay a visit beforehand to quietly observe and acknowledge any thoughts or feelings about the place or situation. Take time to read over the marriage vows beforehand, allowing yourself to grieve over the way they may have been broken in your marriage ending.

While weddings are one-off events, this does not mean attendance is compulsory. My cousin got married three months after we separated. The invitation had arrived at a stage when things were "up in the air". I asked my mum to speak to them and explain a small amount of the situation, and they graciously agreed to wait for our RSVP. Very shortly afterwards we separated, and it would not have been appropriate for my husband to attend. While I would dearly have loved to celebrate with them and my family, I was aware that I couldn't emotionally handle a weekend staying in a hotel with my entire extended maternal family. Saying no to an invitation does not diminish your love for those involved. Arranging to meet and celebrate with them one-on-one, or indeed one-on-two, at an earlier or later date may be an easier way to express your love and joy at their marriage. Sending a card and present also shows your care and consideration, even while you may not feel you can attend.

If you do choose to attend, weddings are a situation where marital status is a topic of conversation – hardly surprising! So be prepared with your answer, unlike me. Being a bridesmaid at a wedding where I knew only a handful of people was helpful. It was about two weeks before we separated for the final time, about six months into this very painful emotional journey. At this event, no one assumed I had an "other half" and those who had known I can only assume were briefed by the bride (a most incredible friend) to not engage in this topic of conversation unless I brought it up. The second event where I knew no one was ten months post decree absolute when I was blind-sided by the question, "Do you have a significant other?" "No, er, I don't." The ultimate answer in eloquent conversation, I cut the conversation dead by accident. It taught me to have a further question prepared, and to rephrase my own questions of others, perhaps asking if they know many others at the wedding instead of enquiring into their relationship status.

Questions to consider

Are you feeling cynical and hardened about marriage? What are some positives about the institution? Focus on the individuals you know getting married and the way they love and show support to one another, rather than thinking of it as an abstract concept.

If you receive an invitation, will you accept? Are there ways to help you manage your own emotions beforehand and on the day itself?

How will you respond if asked about your marital status?

Being in a wedding party

Perhaps the hardest wedding for me to attend was my brother's nuptials. It was in the same church I married in, with my entire family present. My then-husband had decided not to continue our attempts at reconciliation only six weeks before, but we hadn't yet begun the divorce process. My ex was my brother's best friend, as well as my husband, and I was under no illusions that his non-attendance was probably painful for my brother as well. There was never a question of non-attendance in my head: this was *their* day – my brother's wedding – a happy and joyful day. I was happy and joyful for them. To cope, I had several friends primed and ready to text throughout the day. I had been given the option to bring one of these friends but I declined. That said, certain friends lived close to the reception venue and were spending the day at home, ready to walk round to the reception, give me a hug, and send me back in. I spent much of the wedding rehearsal ranting at a friend via text, expressing my anger about my then-husband's disregard of our marriage vows and trying to hold back tears and pain. I hope now that I didn't ruin it, but going to the rehearsal, for me, was the best thing I could have done. Much of the anguish I felt was able to be felt and expressed there, while on the day, hardly anyone heard from me, except for the occasional "Look at the dress!" shot. It was the happiest and most joyful I'd been for a year and a half.

At the wedding in December 2012 where I was a bridesmaid, I was acutely aware of the bride's consideration of me at every point, even drawing me into the circle of her closest friends and inviting me to stay in her family home at the last minute so I wouldn't need to be in a cottage alone. It was very different from my own wedding, which helped, and was a plan I'd been involved in before my marriage broke down. Also, who wouldn't want their best friend to be happy? I knew how much it would mean to her. I was so pleased and happy for her. Feeling less alone as the day approached and being needed to carry out tasks helped to alleviate too much thought and dwell-time.

It is also OK to turn down an invitation to be in the bridal party. Your friend is asking you because of your closeness. Turning it down doesn't mean you don't like them, but that you don't feel able

193

to offer the support before and on the day. If they're as close a friend as the invitation suggests, it's likely they will understand.

Questions to consider

Are there any ways you could be involved to help the couple? Even pouring teas leaves little time for talk and provides you with activity and a chance to escape to the kitchen if it all gets too much.

Are you happy to be involved?

Marriage

Our perception of other people's marriages can also be dramatically impacted by our own. For years after, my suspicions were constantly aroused if a couple seemed to not be talking or spent a considerable amount of time on their phones. Divorce as an experience of marriage can impact how we feel about marriage itself. Is it worth it? Is everyone actually miserable? Can it work? How do people stay together?

People marry confident it is for ever. The wedding day is simply the beginning of the rest of your life. It turns out that divorced or married, your life is never so clear cut as to be mapped out from one event. Maybe you were sold a myth that Christian marriage would be for ever, even if other marriages broke down. Maybe in your culture marriage was the ultimate goal – that you'd "achieved". Yet it ended and you felt you'd been sold a lie. Maybe you married feeling that somehow it wasn't quite right, except it was the "right" thing to do: a logical step and the next part of the relationship. Perhaps now you feel the "right" decision would have been to walk away beforehand, but instead your lives have been torn apart by divorce. This experience can also make weddings hard to fully enjoy and appreciate.

Maybe the thought of getting married again terrifies you. Maybe it appeals and you hope to one day celebrate a long-standing anniversary with another. One thing divorce teaches us about marriage is how hard it is. We know that it's an each and every day commitment. That marriage is routine, the late-night washing up, the ironing. The marriage that's the discussion of finances, what to do next, where to go on holiday. Marriage that's the laying out of true emotions even when they aren't what the other person wants to hear. Some days it might feel worth it. Some days it won't. Marriage is a choice sometimes, a commitment always – and sometimes it can be hard to acknowledge that, for whatever reason, you walked away from it.

Marriage isn't easy. Yours has ended sooner than intended. Even if it had lasted till death parted you, it wouldn't have been perfect; no earthly marriage is.

It's because it isn't easy that I pray for the marriages of those close to me: for their prosperity, communication, and commitment to one another. I want them to thrive in the routine, the unexpected, and the wonderful. Because divorce also teaches us how marriage is worth fighting for, committing to, and how wonderful it can be, yet can only happen with two invested individuals. It's what made us try to keep our marriages whole. It's what makes us hope for that to be true again.

Questions to consider

How do you feel about marriage?

If possible, talk frankly to close friends about their marriage and where they may have experienced difficulty too.

Make a list of three marriages to uphold, pray for, and support. Perhaps offer to do something to enable the couple to spend quality time together.

Christianity and marriage

God's intention for marriage was to portray a mere glimpse of how God loves us: total forgiveness, even at our worst, and being loved regardless. I let God down, He loves me anyway. What a challenge to uphold that in marriage. Marriage is God's covenant to us reflected in an earthly form; marriage I experience on earth will fall short, imperfect as I am.

One major struggle with this is that your marriage has broken down; if this is God's mirror of love on earth how can we end up so broken-hearted? The experience of God, Adam, and Eve in Genesis was the ultimate let down. Adam and Eve had previously walked naked, as vulnerable as we can imagine, together with God in the Garden of Eden. Eve, then Adam, betrayed God – doing the one thing He'd asked them not to do. God knows that broken-heartedness of the one you love dearly rejecting you. It doesn't make it better, but it does bring some comfort that He might know that feeling. Yet still God loved them, and loves us, so much that He sent His only Son to die: "Greater love has no one than this: to lay down one's life for one's friends."[11]

Coping with pregnancy announcements

When my ex-husband and I separated, I was actually glad that my dream of one day having children was as yet unfulfilled; I wouldn't want to have negotiated the pitfalls and devastation of divorce with a child or children to take into account. Conversely, a friend said her children gave her focus and a reason to keep going through her divorce.

For me, the relief of only taking myself into account contrasts to the stamp on broken dreams when someone announces their pregnancy. It can feel like a physical pain. When I was married and held someone's newborn baby, it used to remind me that I didn't

---

11   John 15:13.

want this quite yet, but, I hoped, one day it would happen. Suddenly, there was no us, and all I had was a shattered dream. To mourn the loss of something you didn't have is important. It is the death of a dream.

In our church there was another couple who had been married a similar length of time; I dreaded the moment they would announce their pregnancy. It wasn't that I didn't want them to have a baby – I would have been delighted for them – but it would have been like holding a mirror up to my own life, a "here's what you could have won" moment. Over the years since, I have been privileged to journey and mourn with them in their pain of miscarriage and loss: there is nothing I would love more than to see their scan photos adorn my Facebook wall, or to visit them, holding their treasured little one in my arms. Our perspectives on the lives of others are often skewed by what we are experiencing, and it is worth bearing that in mind as we view what is happening to other people. With pregnancies, childbirth, babies, and children, there is an oft-hidden journey to that point. Perhaps conception has involved many months of crying and pain over periods that arrive bang on time along with dashed dreams that they just haven't shared. Perhaps this has been your own experience too.

Pregnancies are announced through scan pictures on social media in increasingly inventive ways. It is perfectly acceptable to unfollow people or hide those posts if it's too hard. I still liked those people, I was happy for them, but entertaining constant updates of their growing family and obvious love for one another was too much at odds with where I was. I didn't want to unfriend them, but hiding these updates meant I could heal in peace.

While my brother and sister-in-law's wedding had been a joyous day, the moment they announced their pregnancy was incredibly hard personally. I am the eldest sibling. I had always imagined that I would be the first to have children and had always hoped one day to have a daughter – yet now they might have a little girl before me. I was delighted that they were having this much-wanted baby. I was excited to be an aunt, and to meet this new family member. I was also terrified, pain-stricken, and gutted. I would not be the first to present my parents with a grandchild, although I knew this did not mean they would love my hypothetical child any less. I was in a place so far removed from the possibility of having children that my anguish was magnified.

It sounds like jealousy – but I didn't want their baby, I just wanted my own. It sounds like rivalry – it was more the realization that my own expectations were not going to be fulfilled. It sounds like bitterness – I was simply sad, because of what wouldn't be, and of what might never be. I went straight to a friend's after the news and cried and cried, honestly releasing the two conflicting emotions of sheer joy and overwhelming sadness. Only when the sadness was let out, was I able to access the joy for their situation, tinged as it was with my own disappointed hopes.

Before a child is born, the concept of the baby is often much more difficult than the reality. Once my nephew arrived, holding him in my arms I was overwhelmed with love for him. Knowing how much I loved him made the announcement and arrival of my second nephew completely joyful, aided also by the time through which I had begun to heal.

Questions to consider

Do pregnancy announcements jar you? Are there ways to avoid these online?

Do you regularly compare yourself to your peers? Find someone you can speak to about this and ask them to help you identify successes and moments of joy in your own life.

No longer a topic of conversation

In the initial stages, your emotions and experiences may form the content of many conversations you have – whether you want them to or not. If you are an external processor, these conversations can be incredibly helpful, even as they are painful.

As time moves on, these conversations about your situation become fewer and further between. Your "new normal", while feeling abnormal to you, has become "normal" for others. This isn't because they don't care, but because things evolve in their lives too and it is no longer such a surprise. The normality of you no longer being with your spouse happens much more quickly for others – they are not living out the situation every minute of the day. This can feel like a second rejection. It doesn't mean we are not in their thoughts or prayers, but the need for immediate action and support may seem to have passed. Chances are, you are still needing support and this may still be there, but not in the form of regular conversations about your life and where to go next.

Voicing this to others is difficult. We don't want to say that we feel they have forgotten us, but that is exactly how it seems. While our lives revolve naturally around us, everyone else's doesn't and can't. It is a hard transition when for a while the opposite has been true and many people will have been making you a priority in their lives. Even while we feel like we could still have every conversation trying to puzzle out what has happened, there are positives to having wider conversational topics. We may hear more about what our friends are doing or experiencing; we will talk more about other aspects of our lives and perhaps begin to see more of a future for ourselves too.

It may also be that others feel we do not want to be continually asked about how we are doing or feeling or what the current state of play is. They, as well as we, are not mind readers. Unless we tell them we want to be asked or need to make time to talk it through, they will not know. As conversations about ourselves diminish, it also offers us the opportunity to express interest in the lives of others. This is essential to our friendships and may also allow us to help and support others too. Being upfront about a need to talk things through gives our friends the chance to support us, yet hearing about their lives and experiences deepens our friendship too, and allows us to begin looking beyond ourselves and our situations, hard as it is.

Questions to consider

Do you mind that people ask less often about your situation?

What is it about that, that causes the most pain?

Is there a way to express this to your close friends?

Chapter Fifteen

Difficult Dates of the Year

Confronting memories

A friend, now happily remarried for many years, told me the story of going to an event to celebrate a particular achievement of her husband's. The event had been organized by others and was a pinnacle of many years of hard work and determination. As she stood there, heart swelling with pride, she opened her programme – to find that the first song was a song from her first wedding. She shared this with her husband and they laughed over it. There will always be songs, readings, quotes, places that evoke particular memories and emotions.

It was these I found extremely hard. Particular books, locations, and dates evoked memories too difficult to handle initially. When I encountered a book cover, a conversation about a location, a sign on a journey, I could feel the cold spread through my bones like an echo of that fateful day. On advice from a counsellor, I wrote each of these down on separate cards. Nothing was too small or ridiculous to be included – simply anything that raised pain or anger – and I placed them in a flowery tea tin with a clip-close lid. The idea of this activity was to occasionally remove them and confront the words. I could acknowledge my anger or pain and why I felt that way and then put the cards back in the tin, the idea being that one day I would no longer need to do that, because the pain would have diminished.

Having a tin with a clasp helped me as I could physically shut them away.

I wasn't particularly good at removing them as I didn't actually want to confront the anguish and pain I knew they brought out in me. Eventually, I decided to confront one of those cards by deliberately putting myself in the path of the very thing that upset me and made me angry. It wasn't much by many standards – I read a book. And it did upset me. Yet choosing to read it and encounter the emotions connected to it was empowering. The emotion didn't completely go, but it didn't hold the power over me that it once had. The fear of the object was diminished by deliberately putting myself in its path again and choosing to engage with the emotions it held. Rushing into engaging with these things isn't necessary. Take time to encounter the emotions deliberately when you have space and time to process them.

Memories linking to the past can be particularly evocative and stir up powerful, often painful emotions. Managing them is difficult, particularly in the first year or years after separation and divorce where each new date or place is a raw reminder. This chapter seeks to explore some of the pivotal times we may find our new status challenging.

Anniversaries

Celebrate? Commemorate? Commiserate?

How do you respond to an anniversary that's no longer joyous? It was once the happy day of celebration with family and friends, and the future held snuggling under the duvet looking through the photo album and recalling the memories. In years gone by you've booked a holiday, been out for dinner, toasted the day with friends or family and posted a loving (and slightly smushy) Facebook status about the devotion of your spouse. Now the status would involve the cost of divorce, and snuggling under the duvet is because you actually can't bear to face the world outside. The emotions of the celebration are still present, yet heightened in all the wrong ways, and recalling the celebration doesn't have the same happy connotations.

Recalling our wedding, I had my whole married life ahead of me. On the anniversary post-separation, instead of a warm glow emanating from inside, there was a gut-wrenching, crushing reminder that it didn't work out.

Commemorating and acknowledging the anniversary meant a lot of crying, and grieving the loss of the happiest day and the marriage that followed. The first year we acknowledged together the difficult circumstance we were in, and then I hung out with friends. The following year it meant being bolstered by more friends in the light of divorcing. In both circumstances, hanging out with someone who is as happy to talk about your wedding day as to ignore it entirely is incredibly freeing. You aren't having to carefully conceal conflicting emotions about your situation or be unsure whether they will really believe you were happy. They know there was good as well as the bad. It's also helpful when you know them so well, that you know their own marriage has had ups and downs along the way too; they know marriage isn't a breeze. They appreciate yours in its entirety, and are not just commiserating the end.

It is perfectly acceptable to say, "That was actually a great day" – and mean it. I still remember being told it felt like one large family was celebrating on our wedding day, rather than two – making the ultimate split and divorce even harder – but reminding me it was not just me who felt that way. It is valid to acknowledge how happy you were. It is valid to cry tears upon tears. It is just as good to smile and laugh.

Perhaps do something entirely different, that you'd never have done together, to make a new memory. Commemorate the day rather than celebrating it. Commemorating is acknowledging that it was a special day, and now it's a difficult, complicated day, but that you're still here, and probably tougher and stronger than you thought you were.

These same friends can commiserate with you too though. You can do this on your own, but I've found often I need a hug and a bit of perspective. Commiserating is looking back but is also forward-thinking. The end of marriage is the termination of future possibilities as a couple... children, house-buying, holidays, growing old, and getting through tough times together. Those are hard things to lose: a dream always is. And the anniversary is mourning the loss of these precious and long-held dreams. It's being honest about unfulfilment and fears for the future. As you commiserate and commemorate, acknowledge too that this time next year, things will look different, as they will in the years after that too.

That specific date will always be the anniversary of my first wedding. It may be my only wedding anniversary, or it may not be. Each year more of the day passes before I realize, and maybe one day it'll pass by without me noticing it. More lately it has passed without more than a cursory "Oh yes" before my mind continues on with the present-day living. The year my divorce came through, I hosted a ladies' prayer breakfast and spent the remainder of the day singing, dancing, and drinking in the form of *Mamma Mia* and a cocktail bar. My companions were an old friend, a new friend, and someone I'd never met before. For the people who didn't know, there was no need to mention it and to them it was simply another day, but there was someone who got it. We could exchange a knowing look and have a quick hug if suddenly emotions hit and I was finding life hard. I decided that doing something I would enjoy was important and that I would acknowledge the way my life currently was. So I went off to be cheerful with people I didn't know, while watching a play about weddings and love set in a place I would still love to visit – all without crying. That is testament to how far I had come from the day of crying in bed when we had decided to separate.

How did you approach and cope with your wedding and other anniversaries?

Carol: I acknowledged them and allowed myself to be sad for the first one but gradually it became later in the day each time when I realized the date.

Decobe: I suppose in the first few years after the divorce, when various important anniversaries came along I became very solemn and tried everything I could to take my mind off it. As years passed it became much easier. While it no longer causes any pain, I am, after twenty-two years of being on my own, still aware as each anniversary date passes, whether it is the anniversary of my marriage or my ex-spouse's birthday.

Ellie: During our separation we met up on the day that marked our fifth wedding anniversary (eight years together). While I was glad that I could see him on that particular day, it was far from a celebration. By then I had become accustomed to enduring difficult days and I suppose that is what I did: I got through one day at a time. I learned to live in the tension between pain and hope. I knew that if we made it to our sixth wedding anniversary we would probably make it through all other possible ones! By the time that came the following year we were well into the legal process of divorce and I had come to accept that this dream, along with several others, had died. It wasn't what I had chosen – but I focused on the fact that you can't always choose what happens to you but you can choose how you respond.

Christmas

Have you heard of the popular Danish concept of *hygge*? The idea is cosiness, suited to those dark winter months. For me it's the twinkling lights on the Christmas tree in an otherwise darkened

205

room, tucked up under blankets watching a heart-warming film, and indulging in a lot of mulled wine, all coupled with plenty of family card-playing over cups of tea. I love Advent, the waiting and the build-up, coupled with all of these things.

In 2012 December festivities for me were an attempt at normality rather than any actual Christmas cheer. My ex-husband and I separated five days before Christmas. It was unbearable. The emerging traditions, the cosy warmth – all snatched away into a chilling vacuum of Christmas. I slept fitfully at my grandma's house as there was no room at the proverbial inn and I couldn't bear to be by myself in my own home. My entire world was upside down and I had no idea what was going to happen next.

What had originally been planned as a joint family day was spent partly locked in the bathroom, wanting only to sit on the floor, sobbing. Conversation, presents, and joy were palatable for short three- or four-minute bursts before I wanted to scream and hit something. Being surrounded by people was a nightmare, but I didn't want to be by myself. I struggled to think about anyone except myself. I wanted everyone else to enjoy their Christmas, but it was too hard to think beyond myself, my pain, and my loss. Jokes weren't funny, games were irritating, and I was unbelievably on edge. Every conversation seemed ridiculous because it was so insignificant in the turmoil of my world. Trying not to be entirely selfish could only last so long, before I broke down again. Teasing was a no-go, I had no sense of humour and a fuse shorter than my little toe. And when I'm miserable, I don't want to eat.

Christmas can be fraught at the best of times, with timings and gifts, then throw in a devastated relative. Of course no one wants to spend their entire Christmas discussing the whys and wherefores of a trauma, and I was not the only one there. There were seven other people who wanted a happy, family Christmas, with what I can only imagine was a whole combination of feelings about the situation in which they too had been placed, wondering if I would irrationally fly off the handle or be devastated by an insignificant, innocent comment.

During a time that is about family, cuddling up close and picking out presents and decorations, Christmas is a hard time to be alone or to feel lonely. In a family of naturally formed pairs, I've had to acknowledge how lonely I sometimes feel. It's not all romantically attached couples, but their closeness can magnify my own sensation of being alone. Excusing myself to acknowledge those emotions is helpful – allowing myself to disappear off to the bathroom or my makeshift bedroom for a good cry or text a friend. I miss being part of a pair, but now I'm better able to choose when to hold this emotion for later, and when to let the pain out.

It helps to be honest about how fragile you are feeling. Admitting that you think you're going to find it hard frees you up to ask for a hug, or to excuse yourself for fifteen minutes. It is perfectly fine to not be "fine" – to be angry and to be hurting. Being separated or in the middle of an emotional turmoil is, as a colossal understatement, hard, and it's especially hard at Christmas.

I found changing up my traditions helped in the subsequent years, or going back to old family traditions. I didn't think I'd ever wake up in my parents' home again ready for Christmas morning, and the addition of nephews has brought a whole new dimension to Christmases now. Finding new ideas or places to go or things to do stops you from entirely missing what's going on because you're enjoying, or at least experiencing, something brand new.

My few words of wisdom for friends and family of those who are separated are these: laugh with them when they can laugh, mourn and cry with them when they cry, accept those moments when they're angry, and reassure them you'll be there when the future seems bleak.

We survived that Christmas, somehow, and all returned the following year. Time had left the wound less raw, though still agonizing and sore to touch. But the particular memory I have now of that "first" Christmas is that, amid the loneliness, there was love. Not the love I was desperately missing, but a long-lasting, well-established acceptance of anything I was feeling. Love that tolerated my inability to eat and my constant urge to cry; love that tolerated my snapping, mood-swings, and the fact that it was too painful to watch a Christmas film. It was an unconditional, deep-rooted love from my childhood that was given without question, despite me and because of me. It was a love that would have done anything to soak up my pain and make things well for me. It's the same love, I believe, that sent Jesus to earth that first Christmas.

I am thankful for their gifts of time, of patience, and of generosity. Even six years on, writing this, it is hard not to cry. Not because I am still amidst that turmoil, but because I have the deepest and most heartfelt gratitude to the people who kept me going that Christmas. And who, at my most unlovable and feeling at my most unloved, loved me, and continue to love me, without question or expectation. As ever, these might not be the people we expect to be there, but gradual healing can happen with those with whom we find acceptance.

Questions to consider

How do you feel about Christmas?

Are there traditions you can change or adapt so that the difference is less palpable?

Where will you spend Christmas?

Will you have your own room and opportunity to leave the room and be alone if it becomes too much?

Where do you feel loved at Christmas? How has this or might this sustain you through a challenging festive period?

New Year

I've long had a particular struggle with New Year. Aside from the overwhelming urge to go to sleep at around 11:15 p.m. (with only forty-five minutes to go it seems defeatist at this point), the TV programming that is never entertaining enough for me, and the anticlimax at 12:11 a.m. once the fireworks are ended, there's a key element I don't like: "Ooh, what's going to happen this year?"

I don't know! I don't like not knowing! I have *never* liked not knowing!

To my mind there is only an enormous sense of trepidation, combined with a dread of all the horrendous things that could happen. What if, what if, what if? My brain goes into overdrive. Maybe I would be better off getting an early night.

But if the past few years have taught me anything, it's that you can never know what will happen, not happen, or turn out differently. You can never plan for the year ahead in the way you might like, although intentions and dreams are worthy and useful. I don't imagine a single one of us reading this anticipated our marriage would end like this, or that separation would happen. Particularly in this case, the not knowing, and the stretch of 365 days of unknowing, is incredibly disconcerting. But as a certain someone (Jesus) wisely said, each day has enough troubles of its own.[12] So don't be tempted to borrow the troubles from December before January has begun!

A challenge of January is to believe that something good and exciting might happen over the coming year. If I can find something pleasant and enjoyable in each day, even in the third week of January; if I can think of things I might do, and imagine that there might be other opportunities awaiting me, I can begin to see the unknown as possibility instead of intimidation.

---

12   Matthew 6:34.

We may begin the New Year desperate for reconciliation. We may hope for a restoration of our marriage and the love there was once between us. We may begin it hoping to move on and build a new start. However we start it, we can have one thing in common. Make plans that depend on you without having to rely on your ex-spouse to pull through on something. Not only does this mean you aren't disappointed by them, possibly again, but that you are empowered too. It doesn't have to be a big goal! Cooking yourself dinner, cleaning the bathroom, reorganizing the bookshelf. In a way, the purpose isn't the task itself, it is the achievement at the end of it.

We can often be confident that the year will not end looking as it did at the start. Personal growth, spiritual growth, relocation, a new room layout, and changed marital status are just a few of the many ways in which your year could change. Trying to look ahead to the end doesn't help us, as we can't anticipate the future, but instead we can take slight comfort in the change and evolution of the year to ensure we won't be exactly where we are now when the year ends.

Questions to consider

How does New Year make you feel?

What did you anticipate the last New Year to look like? Be realistic with yourself about disappointed hopes and expectations, as well as any positive surprises such as friends who were there for you.

What small goal could you achieve independently this year?

Valentine's Day

Ah, the celebration of love. We can argue it's forced, commercialized, and we should just express love every other day of the year. But, however we dress it up, Valentine's Day can be monumentally successful at making you feel alone and unloved.

Your experience of Valentine's Day with no partner may mirror the experience of someone who never realized the dream of being a parent on Mother's or Father's Day. The expectation and focus on that particular type of love heightens your awareness of not receiving it. It is hard not to dwell on the past when we did have this romantic love, whether or not it was expressed on 14 February, or to wonder whether someone will ever love us in this way again. Both are lonely places to be, magnifying the negative emotions.

Conversely, it may be that you experience relief at not needing to pretend any longer and manufacture a love you are not feeling. Perhaps you are glad not to be the recipient of that love and expectation from a person you didn't want to care for you.

As with anniversaries, choosing to spend the day in a deliberate way, whether that is making the choice to have a day under the duvet or making a plan out of the house, gives a different focus to what you might otherwise have been doing.

There are many other ways to view love to help us feel less alone. We may be romantically unattached but there are many ways to feel love and to be loved. It can be hard to bear this, feeling as you might the loss of the romantic, steady love you had come to rely on. But the other loves exist and are sometimes the way we can be sure that love is not entirely gone from life. Siblings, parents, children, nieces and nephews, cousins, pets, others in the community; there are a myriad of ways that love is expressed, given, and received. These are no less a form of love than romantic love, so choosing to acknowledge these is healthy and positive and reminds you of those who love you and whom you love. This is not to ignore the grief you may be feeling. As with other anniversaries, this anniversary of love is a time to grieve the love that we have lost. Yet choosing to acknowledge in one small way the love that has been shown to you also accepts that love exists; that it's not over because one love has been lost.

Questions to consider

What will you plan for Valentine's Day?

Can you make a list of those whom you love?

Is there an encouraging way you could express love to someone? Write to a friend or show your nieces, nephews, or children how much they are loved.

The pain of anniversaries and memories remains, but time does dull it. They pass by as places on a map, items around the house, and dates on the calendar, where the occasional remembrance springs to mind. Getting through the first of all these experiences is doubtless the hardest. Be kind to yourself and allow yourself space to think and feel as you want and need to.

Which "big" event did you find hardest, and how did you endure and eventually enjoy it?

Carol: I'm not sure I found them hard; they had been harder while married due to my ex's drinking. Instead it was a relief and nice to enjoy celebrations knowing they wouldn't be spoiled… I started to build nice memories instead of marred ones.

Decobe: I think Christmas was the most difficult time for me after the divorce. Thankfully, I have only ever experienced one Christmas totally on my own since the divorce, and that was agony. Nowadays, Christmas is always spent either with my daughter and her family, or with one or both of my brothers.

Ellie: Rather than avoid difficult and poignant times, my approach was to meet them head on. I celebrated my birthday, Christmas, and New Year with purpose, but also with what I hope was a dignity and honesty that acknowledged how difficult things were, and yet determined to make the most of life. I hosted Christmas for the first time at my flat with just my immediate family. I cooked everything from scratch including Christmas cake and Christmas pudding, which kept me busy. During our separation I turned thirty. I decided to have a cocktail party but instead of hosting a big crowd in a hall, I invited twenty good friends who understood my situation to my place to enjoy cocktails and cupcakes together. To have something positive to focus on, I set myself a challenge of completing thirty new challenges or experiences in my year of being thirty. During that year I had afternoon tea at the Ritz and flew a helicopter!

May: I forgot the wedding anniversaries as we were only married a short time. Christmas is a hard one but I either spend time with my brother's family or with friends. I once spent Christmas with the homeless serving food, which I enjoyed doing. For my birthday I try to arrange something my friends will also enjoy.

Strategies for difficult dates

Refocus the day on to another event. Perhaps this day has another connotation to focus on. It might be a friend's birthday, a sporting event, or just a "normal" day. When a friend revealed to me that my wedding day had been the same date as her father's funeral I was very apologetic, as she had also had a role in the wedding itself. However, it had given the day a different focus for her, and while it could still hold painful memories, those were gradually replaced with new ones. The same would be true for me too.

Plan in advance how you will spend the day. Will it be alone? Will you meet friends? Are there specific times of day that are difficult for you? If so, make sure you have made plans around that particular time. If you know you will just want to curl up in pyjamas, watch films, and eat sweets all day, find a friend who is also happy to devote their day to those activities, and who will go with the flow of the day.

Make yourself the priority by doing something your ex-spouse would not have wanted to do. Is there somewhere you've been meaning to go to or something you wanted to do or learn? This is a great opportunity to feel liberated to do that. He or she wasn't necessarily holding you back before, but now you can embrace this chance to make a new achievement or memory.

Praise and reward yourself for making it through the morning, or a difficult time of day. It is not easy. So give yourself credit for the achievement of making it through that painful time.

The same strategies and approach can apply to unhappy anniversaries too. Perhaps the day the divorce was finalized, or the day you found out your marriage was over. Maybe these are celebratory, maybe they're not; only you will know how the day might make you feel, yet those emotions may yet take you by surprise. Roll with the emotions the day brings, accepting them all as valid ways to feel, even the surprising ones.

Rowena's story

I got married in 1986 when I was nineteen. He was in the army while we were dating, and found out that he was due to be posted to Germany. You had to be married to go and live in Germany with a soldier, so that's what we did. It probably wasn't the best of reasons, and we probably married too quickly. We had known each other for about a year when we decided to get married. We had been married for six years when we split up, and we divorced shortly after that. It was all a long time ago now, and it's a bit hazy in the memory. In some ways it seems like another lifetime, and not part of my life at all now.

At the time it was awful. We had financial problems at times as he was addicted to gambling, so trust was an issue. He did a six-month tour in Cyprus, so I left my job in Germany and spent ten weeks of that six months in Cyprus with him. I returned to my parents' home in the UK for what would have been the rest of the tour, as I didn't want to be in Germany on my own with no job. However, he phoned me from Cyprus on my return, having spent all that time there, to say that he wanted a divorce. There was no explanation and had been no mention of it while I had been with him. He expected me to stay at my parents' house and not return to Germany. (Spoiler: I didn't.)

We both returned to Germany, and after much talking and getting nowhere, we stayed in the flat together in separate rooms. It was torturous. We tried marriage guidance counselling, but this coincided with the start of the Gulf War, which he went off to. The counsellor wasn't keen on picking apart all the trauma and emotions of our marriage when he was about to go off to war and potentially not coming back, so I was left to deal with my own trauma and emotion.

I got another job in Germany and stayed for four months or so until they came back from the Gulf. During this time I discovered he was seeing someone, and had been while he was in Cyprus. For me this was the point of no return, so I accepted that the marriage was over. I returned to England and moved into our house, which we had been renting out, with a good friend to help pay the rent. Divorce followed soon after that.

I am now happily married and we are coming up to our twenty-fifth wedding anniversary.

Chapter Sixteen

Intimacy

What do we mean by intimacy?

Isn't this what we have longed for? We are created as sexual beings, and it is a gift given to us by God to enjoy.

But perhaps it has been missing from your marriage for a long time. Or perhaps now it's suddenly been snatched away through separation, and you're left with a deep longing for love and intimacy.

The Bible wisely instructs to not awaken love until the appropriate time, but what do you do with a love already awoken and a desire for another that must now remain unfulfilled?

Sex, and missing sex, is one of the major aspects of a marriage that is swept under the carpet when we speak about divorce. It is this physical intimacy that distinguishes and sets apart our romantic relationships. When you're close enough to another divorcee to discuss this, they will freely acknowledge how difficult it is to suddenly be without this. It is entirely normal to miss sex.

That said, it's a challenging topic to bring up in a coffee shop, and one that appears to expose your vulnerabilities. In British culture, frank chats about sex aren't often the norm. But when I've summoned up the courage to mention this, others have laughed in agreement. They've not laughed at my question, but rather at the acknowledgment that this is one of the major, unspoken difficulties around being divorced. So feel free to say that you miss sex! Feel free to say that you *don't* miss sex. Maybe you miss the intimacy, the emotional, spiritual, physical, and chemical connections from your marriage. In this section we're going to explore a number of ways we might negotiate the missing of and yearning for these intimacies, and how we can find fulfilment in healthy ways while being separated and divorced.

What did you miss most about being married?

Carol: Somebody else being in the house when I got home. And watching the Formula 1 while eating Sunday dinner! Also, I had to give up my dog to my ex as I was out too long during the day to care for him properly. I made the decision when a "friend" who was supposed to let him out at lunchtime obviously didn't. He had been indoors for thirteen hours without a wee, and it broke my heart!

Decobe: The thing I miss the most is companionship and having someone to come home to, and to be able to share mine and their day's experiences.

Ellie: What I missed most was just being with him. I lost my best friend and missed the intimacy that you have in marriage: physical, emotional, and spiritual. Certain little things reminded me of this and emphasized a feeling of emptiness; for example, coming home to our flat without him there or going to sleep in our bed alone. It wasn't as much that I was on my own, as it wouldn't have bothered me if he'd been away briefly for a different reason. Rather it was the lack of his presence during those circumstances that highlighted he might not ever come back. He was the person

I would chat to if anything else in life was difficult, and facing it together made all the difference. So it was incredibly hard not just to not have him around, but also to accept that he was the reason for my heartache, and he was choosing to treat me like that.

May: I miss companionship and being with someone I can love; someone to chat to when I get in from work and share a meal with, too.

Rowena: When I still lived in the same flat as him, I missed the fact that we were no longer best friends and could just hang out.

What is physical intimacy?

When physical intimacy inside your marriage is not available, it can be tempting to seek this elsewhere. The first question to address is: what is it that we miss? As a shortlist:

- *expressing love*
- *fun*
- *physical closeness*
- *emotional closeness*
- *feeling loved*
- *orgasm*
- *feeling fulfilled*
- *being able to give another that fulfilment*
- *feeling desired and attractive*
- *expressing desire for your partner*
- *a sign of commitment and covenant*

And this list probably doesn't even scratch the surface – it's something to be experienced rather than listed! Everyone's experiences will be different, will have changed, and each will miss different things about it. You might not miss all these things all the time.

It is good to become aware of what you're missing when you feel that desire for physical intimacy. Are you missing the physical closeness of another person? Do you want to feel attractive to someone else? Do you want to just have sex or orgasm? Being able to more easily pinpoint what you are craving and what you miss may also help you to lay that desire down and acknowledge exactly where you're feeling tempted, as well as crying, "I just miss sex!"

There is nothing that will take the place of everything we miss about that sexual relationship, save for a future sexual relationship (though that is not a reason to rush into one!) Sleeping with a relative stranger or even a friend, might provide some of the physical closeness and enjoyment of sex, but not the commitment. Pornography is no substitute for true intimacy and is an exploitative industry, designed to prey on our desire for intimacy or sex, while not fulfilling either. Even simply kissing people on nights out will never completely fulfil the need to feel desired and attractive.

Separation and divorce involves a physical, emotional, and spiritual separation from your one sexual partner. You have given your heart, your body and exposed yourself in full vulnerability to this person, only to have them disregard these gifts and trample them underfoot. I do not diminish this pain, but a new sexual relationship is not the salve for this pain. Sure it may make you feel good for a period of time, but this gratification is not the lasting commitment and deep understanding for which your soul is searching.

First of all, you need to work through that broken trust, self-esteem, and vulnerability that make you want to put up a guard. If you're a Christian, you could ask God to begin healing these issues you are facing. But healing from these deep hurts may also come through other people's encouragement or dependability. By seeking God's healing, we also begin to seek intimacy with Him, as we bring our deepest and most heartfelt issues to Him.

We also need to find healthy forms of physical closeness. Physical closeness releases endorphins into our bodies. If you miss this, find friends who like hugs! If your love language[13] is touch, hugs can be a life-restoring action. Being held and supported for an extended period of time is so helpful. You will find people you can hug without agenda and who will hold you until you feel restored. Make the most of it; they will want to support you and love you, and they're probably feeling better from a hug too.

Questions to consider

What situations and timings cause you to miss physical intimacy?

Does viewing romantic storylines make you crave physical intimacy?

Are you seeking physical intimacy in any ways that you feel are unhealthy? Who are you going to speak to about these and what are you going to do?

Do you have a friend you can hug?

Are there any parts of your physical past to repent of or seek healing for?

Intimacy with God

"But God," you may be crying, "I followed all the rules! I followed your instructions to the letter!" The unfairness of having kept sex for marriage, only to have your partner leave, may feel particularly harsh.

I think God loves that you did this. He loves that you wanted to follow His guidance, given to protect your heart. Whatever your

---

13 As described in *The Five Love Languages* by Dr Gary Chapman, Moody Press, 2015.

past sexual experiences before marriage, God does not condemn us. He may convict us, and we need to ask for forgiveness to heal fully, but there is no condemnation in Christ Jesus. Whatever your past experience, you have ended in a place of pain and anguish, that you may have thought you were protected from.

God gives us guidance on the ideal circumstances for physical relationships for a reason: to stop us from experiencing hurt. However, He has never promised us immunity. It is easy to forget that all areas of our lives are susceptible to trouble, difficulties, and persecution. The devil comes to steal, kill, and destroy. The Bible does not say that this excludes our marriage relationship. In fact, as an earthly comparison of the way God feels about us, perhaps we should be more fully aware of the devil's determination to destroy marriage and to kill the sanctity and love of the relationship.

Intimacy is defined as being closely acquainted, or as having a detailed and thorough knowledge. Our desire for intimacy can be met in God. This might not feel like great news, even if we're Christians, or you might not believe in God at all. What we miss is a physical closeness, a presence, and a human person beside us to talk to: intimacy with God doesn't often offer these things. But we can become closely acquainted with God. Like a parent and a child, He already knows us yet longs to talk to us, that we might come to know Him better. Intimacy is created when people spend time with what they want to learn more about. In sex it is exploring one another, but it is just as applicable to exploring and understanding a theoretical concept or a piece of software!

Our first, most long-lasting relationship of intimacy should be with God. Intimacy with Him shouldn't feel like a second best. In fact, at every point of our lives – single, married, or divorced – intimacy with God should be our first desire, above intimacy with our spouse. Placing our spouse first, putting sex on a pedestal, or dating a partner before investing in our relationship with God is not a good move. The great news is that we can shift our focus back to God. But, coming from a married and now divorced/single perspective – I can see what Paul means when he says singleness gives more time to pursue God!

Intimacy with God means spending time with Him, rather than seeking out our next relationship to fulfil us. Using time to invest in that relationship and learn what God has to say about us may help to prevent us seeking the balm of another person and potentially being hurt further by someone who isn't committed to us. Use the new time you've been given to explore who God is, and who He says you are.

Questions to consider

How do you view intimacy with God?

Have you placed your marriage, spouse, or something within your marriage on a pedestal above God?

Where do we seek intimacy?

It could be tempting after the marriage has ended to pursue someone else who finds us attractive as a means of bolstering our self-esteem, without having any real intentions toward them. It may be tempting to sleep with someone, in order to experience that physical closeness and the fulfilment of sex. It could be tempting to watch pornography or read overtly sexual literature in order to feed that desire for intimacy or sex. It might be tempting to have many in-depth conversations with someone of the opposite gender, even knowing they are married or in a relationship, in order to experience that emotional closeness.

These are by no means abnormal feelings. The desire for intimacy in all its guises has been awoken in you and that was good and appropriate. But now, in separation and divorce, we must consciously choose to pursue healthy outlets for these desires. We need to be ready to guard against any inappropriate expressions of these desires outside of marriage. If your marital breakdown and even your own actions have taken us by surprise, so too can the temptation to deepen our conversations and time with others with whom it may not be appropriate.

It can be very simple expressions of intimacy that we notice we are missing. Have you ever seen a couple glance at one another across a room, somehow speaking to each other with their expressions? I think this is one of the greatest intimacies in a deep relationship, including friendship, and it is one of the things I missed a great deal. There is the intimacy of knowing someone's prior self, or their backstory; the intimacy of knowing the bits they don't like about themselves that they've let you see anyway. There are a thousand different ways to experience this depth of relationship with another person, and it is magnified in marriage.

Focusing on friendships where you can be open, honest, tactile, and share life experiences builds intimacy. These could be with friends or family members – intimacy isn't simply about sex; it's about someone else knowing the real you. When they know and love the real you, it is healing to a soul that's been wounded by rejection.

Questions to consider

What intimacies from your marriage do you miss the most?

Is there an intimacy that was missing with your spouse, or that you felt was somehow lacking?

How will you grieve these?

Where do you seek intimacy first?

Are you seeking out unhealthy opportunities to fill that void? Who will you share this struggle with?

What circumstances heighten your desire for intimacy?

Do you miss emotional, physical, or spiritual intimacy most?

Switched off from sex

It may be that your ex-spouse has been intimate with another person. I'm not using this as a euphemism – there is much more to sex and making love than intercourse, and a whole range of infidelities can damage a marriage. This can make the thought of intimacy incredibly difficult. Were comparisons made? What happened there that didn't happen with me? Am I not attractive, sexy, or interesting enough? Simply – am I not enough?

There are two separate issues here: your spouse and their actions and your own feelings towards sex and self-worth.

I think loss of self-worth and self-esteem are two of the major challenges to battle when adultery or intimacy with another person has broken up the marriage. Remembering that no single person can fulfil all another's needs is helpful. It's why we have different friends who we may turn to for different things. It's why, in relationships, it's important not to neglect our friendships and those whom we love.

Simply because someone has cheated on you does not mean you are lacking. Yes, you will never be able to be everything to one person – and that's healthy; that's OK. The fact that they have chosen to look outside the marriage for the emotional or physical intimacy they wanted is not. But that is not because you were lacking somehow. You being you is highly unlikely to have been a justifiable reason for their actions: those were still their choices.

It may be that your anger around infidelity is unjustifiably directed more at one person in this situation than the other. Anger itself is justifiable; our actions may not be. It was much easier for me to feel angry at someone I didn't know than at my ex, yet, in my situation, both were culpable.

Going out and sleeping with someone else wasn't going to solve my problem of feeling inadequate and rejected when it came to sex. Counselling and exploring why I felt the way I did about my ex's and my own attitudes to sex were the things I found to be helpful. I had learned reactions, as we naturally do, from the circumstances I was in and therefore needed to work out where these came from and how to gradually unpick and move past these. Grounding myself in the present helped considerably, as well as working out why and how I had felt rejected and why that was problematic in marriage. Marriage is the ideal place for a sexual relationship, so any damage caused to that can be quite profound in our reactions to sex. If you find your reactions seem extreme or unreasonable, I would suggest seeking counselling support to unpick what can be a very complex, emotive issue that can be difficult to talk about honestly.

Questions to consider

Are you switched off from sex because of your ex's or your own actions?

How do you react to someone declining sex?

What are you seeking in having sex with someone else?

Do you need to seek help to explore the way your mind has learned to respond to sex or the idea of it?

Emotional intimacy

The in-depth discussions of emotions, dreams, goals, and hopes is a healthy and helpful part of marriage. Your spouse was likely to have been, at one time, your deepest confidante. A bitter irony of separation and divorce is the absence of this one person you would wish to share all of those deepest thoughts and feelings with.

Finding someone to have these conversations with is incredibly valuable. It might not have been the people you most expected to converse with, but these friends will become those who can challenge you, cry with you, and celebrate with you as you move through separation and divorce. Find those who can pray with you, and for you, and who form community with you.

Because of the nature of the conversation, perhaps confessing sin, secrets, or personal dreams and disappointments, it might be helpful that some of the people you speak with are not of the same gender as your ex-spouse, or even that you meet with a couple. This might sound silly. Perhaps you find it easier to talk to someone of the same gender as your ex. But already in a place of emotional fragility, there is potential for us to develop a dependency or relationship that unintentionally begins to take the place of our married relationship. The implications of forming this relationship unknowingly, or before we have healed from our prior hurts and habits, has the potential to hurt us or them. There is nothing wrong with having friends. It is likely though that what you are missing is a deep emotional connection with your ex; someone with whom you can talk through some of life's complexities and the issues you may be battling. Replacing this with a deepening friendship that could develop into attraction is unlikely to help us solve these problems, and may cause us, or others, further hurt.

Again, we need to consider our own motivations. Does this conversation satisfy a need in us to engage deeply with someone? Is the friendship helping us to feel attractive or worthwhile when they seek us out to speak to us? Are we looking forward to speaking to that one person significantly more than others? Friendships aren't unhealthy in themselves, but we can be wise and self-aware in order to communicate well at a time when we are very emotionally vulnerable.

Questions to consider

When you are seeking physical, emotional, or spiritual intimacy with someone, consider these questions:

If you had a partner, what would their reaction to this be?

Do they have a partner? If so, would you discuss these issues with them/spend time with them in the same way?

Are your conversations and actions helpful and appropriate to upholding their marriage or relationship?

When do your conversations take place? If they are late at night, consider the implications for each of you, particularly if they have a partner.

If roles were reversed, what would you consider their expectations and intentions to be?

Did you know them well before, or has this relationship begun/deepened because of your divorce?

What are your motivations?

Divorce can suddenly remove physical, emotional, and spiritual intimacy. How did you negotiate this loss?

Carol: I didn't have it during my marriage so I didn't have to negotiate it, but I actually began building this with friends and life group when I started going back to church.

Decobe: The three types of intimacy are very different to each other. Spiritual intimacy proved to be no problem; it actually got much better in the years after the divorce, as I grew closer to God. Emotional intimacy was a bit harder, but thankfully I had two children who needed to be loved and I was able to share my emotional side with them. Regarding physical intimacy, this was never a problem as it had been sadly lacking during the married years, so was no real great loss. It's amazing that I have two children!

Ellie: This made me feel desperately sad at the beginning because no one else could fulfil that in the same way, and also I was aware that it would take a long time to rebuild those things even if we did get back together. What helped me enormously was finding that I could be brutally honest with God about how I was feeling, and then listen and find a peace that I couldn't explain. Some particular friends and my sisters also helped by listening to me talk endlessly about the situation, understanding that it consumed my life at that point. They gave me the time and space to express how I was feeling and what I was thinking, supporting me without judging me.

May: My ex lent me an exercise bike so I tried to keep fit and I enjoy doing sports too. I think being creative: painting or playing a musical instrument helps with the emotional and spiritual loss.

Rowena: Emotionally and physically it was hard to start with, but when the person you have had those things with no longer wants to share them with you, you begin to change your attitude toward wanting it with them and just adapt.

Chapter Seventeen

New Beginnings

New relationships

There are many suggestions and ideas on when it is ideal to begin a new relationship. I felt I had grieved much of my marriage by the time the divorce came through. Theoretically, if I had met someone new at that point, to an outsider it would have looked to have happened extremely quickly, whereas to me it would have actually happened after three years of separation, grieving, and moving on. I didn't actually start a new relationship then. But only we can know when we are ready for a new relationship.

Part of this is understanding and appreciating where you are with relationships. If your main thoughts are of your ex, perhaps you're not ready – they may still preoccupy your mind leaving no space for a new partner.

There are many different ways in which our past experiences may impact on our new relationships. Being aware of the potential thought patterns, assumptions, and fears we bring with us can help us go some way to addressing them. Once again, it may be that we need to seek professional help. We cannot rely on a new partner to smooth over the cracks of our past or to mend our thought processes. In brief, we may struggle with trust, fear, intimacy, commitment, jealousy. Unfortunately, as with any life experience, there are likely to be ways that our brain processes things which may not be completely accurate but are born out of those situations. If you are finding this or are aware that it may one day become a problem, you may wish to start taking those thoughts captive. Scientists suggest that the more we think a thought, the deeper the natural course it takes, much like a meandering river. However, when we begin to notice these thoughts, we can redirect them. It's challenging. We have to identify the thought, explain to ourselves internally how it isn't true, and replace it with truth.

Questions to consider

Are there any persistent thoughts that arise from your experience of separation and divorce?

Do you feel realistically ready to date again?

One potential excitement and joy we can look forward to amidst divorce is that we may one day experience that thrill of new love again. I never imagined I would have a new partner – and I was perfectly content with that! Yet divorce does offer us the opportunity, one day, to find love again. In part, this is daunting but also an exciting opportunity.

Well-meaning friends will sometimes encourage us to date, and to look to the future in this way, but there are many ways we can look ahead, as we explore in this final section. Replacing one romantic relationship with another is not the primary way forward, and definitely doesn't mean life will be rosy again. Becoming complete by ourselves is the foremost concern for many of us in the initial stages of separation and divorce. We can remain sure that liking ourselves and who we are is a fantastic way to begin a new relationship, should that happen, and either way brings us contentment and the ability to be confident in our individual selves.

Who am I now?

When we develop a relationship there is a big change in our identity and in how we identify ourselves. We become someone's husband or wife, an in-law and perhaps a parent or step-parent. Gradually, we adopt personality traits of our partner and our identity is forged by their likes and dislikes too. We might eat particular foods or go to particular places on holiday. We might pick up their attitudes towards things and find that they're beginning to influence our own ideas and opinions. In marriage, we become half of a whole, while hopefully remaining true to ourselves. Our marriage partner is there to complement us, not complete us.

But if, like me, you got married young, you became part of a couple without ever experiencing adulthood alone. Alone is therefore a very scary place to be. Even if you were single for a time as an adult, suddenly finding yourself in that place again is incredibly difficult. By then you have invested in your relationship, grown together, and worked toward a whole that is now split in two. Because of the length of time you've been together or the intensity of relationship, it can often feel that your spouse has completed you, so that in separation you have become less of a whole person.

I didn't really know who I was without my ex. I'd never been an adult without him. I'd been to university without him, and I remembered enjoying that, but our relationship was a bedrock of my life then, as it had been since. I didn't know how to be by myself: I'd never lived by myself – *ever*. I didn't know where to turn; I'd always turned to him. If I was truly honest, I'd lost "me" in being part of "us". Our relationship formed the basis of my whole life. While I sometimes did those things I loved, I had become easily swallowed into the routine and the joint ventures. When we separated, I had no idea even what music I liked. My ex was very musical and so we had tended to listen to what he liked. That wasn't to say I liked it necessarily – and occasionally we did listen to my nineties' pop – but my musical tastes weren't at the fore.

You may feel confident that you still know yourself outside of the marriage and that you never lost that essence of yourself that others seem to. If so, well done – and please write to me and tell me how! Knowing who you are is challenging, and loving who you are when someone else has chosen not to is even more so.

An essential part of separation and divorce is learning to rediscover and even like yourself. So, how we can rediscover ourselves and our identities to become whole, rounded, independent people, who will not be lost in a future relationship? It's a process that takes time. Loving ourselves while someone else doesn't can be incredibly difficult. But rediscovering who we are, what we like, and that we're interesting people makes a world of difference.

Questions to consider

Did or do you feel you lost yourself in marriage?

Write down three things you know you like. Reflect on these; what is it about them that brings you joy? Is there any way you can bring more of these into your life at the present time?

When was the moment you "knew" you'd be OK?

Carol: After church one day, having spent the whole service in tears: I felt much lighter.

Rowena: I'm not sure I ever thought I wouldn't be. I tend to deal with situations in the moment and not think long-term.

Ellie: At one point in one of the many discussions we had while separated, I told my then husband that if we divorced I

232

would never be OK. I think what I meant was that deep down I knew I would never be the same and I would have to live with the consequences of our relationship breakdown, which I do. However, I have recovered well; not just surviving but thriving. The knowing I'd be OK moment came when I was out running one evening. I was thinking about what to say to someone about my situation at the time. We were separated and I wasn't certain what the eventual outcome would be. I realized that I was learning to be content whatever the circumstances, and I remember thinking that I didn't know if we'd end up back together and have 2.4 children or if we'd split up and face the unknown. But I had hope either way.

May: I never knew if I would be OK – I just tried to survive: I got some satisfaction from my work, kept some friendships, enjoyed walking and sailing.

Interests and hobbies

While divorce can easily feel like it has robbed us of much, it also has the capacity to give us a great deal and to broaden our opportunities and horizons. Without a spouse to discuss our choices with, we are free to make our own choices. That, however, can be a daunting task. There are no limits, which is simultaneously a place full of excitement and of fear. Where do you even begin to establish what you like and don't like again?

We may have pursued hobbies and interests with our spouse. For some, it may be inappropriate or impossible to continue with those things and we may begin to flounder because that former outlet of emotion or joy is no longer available to us. Sometimes even when going it alone, we will have had our ex's support around us so the prospect of entering a room of strangers alone is daunting and possibly inhibiting.

Rediscovering who I was and what I liked were processes that worked in tandem. As I rediscovered things I'd previously enjoyed, and some experiences I'd never had, I began to feel more confident in myself and who I was. Since realizing I hardly ever listened to my own music, I began to discover songs I liked. Discovering that I had a musical taste was liberating. It might not have been a highbrow taste, or at all distinctive, but it was *my* taste in music. I also found that I could simply sit and read – my ex hadn't really enjoyed reading, so although we'd spend time doing different things, me being able to sit in bed and read for three hours on a Saturday morning was an experience I had missed.

Learning about who I was also meant I had the opportunity to change and to learn about ways I had changed too. As my ex-husband had disliked flying, and I had been plain scared of it, we had decided not to stress ourselves out through flying on holiday, preferring to travel by train, boat, or car. Once we had divorced, I decided that I would challenge myself to undertake a fear of flying course; in fact, this very sentence was written on a balcony in Crete overlooking the sea – a holiday I'd never have undertaken with my ex for a myriad of reasons.

One of the most effective strategies I employed in 2014 was to write a list of 100 things to do. The plan was that I would have a list of things to achieve in the midst of waiting (at this stage we had been separated for twelve months with no end in view), while helping me to work out some things I thought I had missed or thought I might like. I threw everything on to my list, until it contained pretty much anything I hoped to achieve. Some of the dreams felt (and were) entirely unrealistic, some were trivial, and others felt colossal. The goals needed to bring me alive again. They needed to help me explore who I was as an individual. By writing a list of all the things I enjoyed doing, I began to remind myself of who I was, meaning I ended the year able to answer questions like "What music do you like?" Or,

"How would you spend a perfect day?" with my own considered opinion.

Nothing was too trivial to make it on to the list; in fact, a few trivial goals were straightforward and easy to tick off. Framing a picture, drinking more water, painting my nails, and travelling by train went on the list.

I played more cards, lay on the beach looking for shooting stars, and I sang my heart out in the car in front of (selected) friends. I went to a gig, the dancing show I used to perform in as a child, a musical, a comedy show, a football (soccer) match, and the Victoria and Albert Museum in London. I discovered I don't really like art galleries and like to march around museums at pace. I'd also entirely forgotten how I actually very much enjoy sitting on a hard, plastic seat in the cold to watch football.

Every goal was about me. None of them depended on anyone else doing anything; I could have gone about them all independently. This was incredibly helpful. I could invite a friend to join me, and one did involve a particular pre-discussed holiday, but my aim was to be able to achieve them regardless of relationship status or friend availability. The goals weren't entirely selfish though, and a significant number involved communicating more regularly and fully with family and friends, and paying visits.

My primary goal was to go to London for an evening because I knew London brought something in me alive. Never would I have added "getting a job in" or "move to" London to my list. I can't even remember now when I went for an evening specifically, or what I did, but I imagine I thoroughly enjoyed it at the time.

Now, of course, this isn't the only way to rediscover who you are. But the list made me feel alive again. My love of live performance (in whatever guise) was reignited. I began writing again – little imagining that a few years on I'd be writing a book. Perhaps the best way to sum up my 2014 is in one simple sentence: I felt alive again.

Perhaps you'd like to explore different facets of your life, maybe once a month. For your birthday ask people to fill a jar with experience ideas or gift you a second-hand book to read or album to listen to, so as to begin to broaden your horizons.

Questions to consider

Can you list three things you have always wanted to do within an accessible distance of where you live?

Did you stop pursuing a particular hobby because of your spouse? Can you reignite that enjoyment now?

What's in a name?

Names are a crucial part of our identity, and on marriage names are often changed to reflect this occasion. You may have double barrelled your names together; you may have kept your name; your spouse may have taken your name; maybe you created your own – there is a wealth of options. Often the assumption is that the female will take the male surname, although increasingly this is not always the case. So what happens to your name when you divorce?

For those who've changed their name, divorce triggers questions about whether or not to change their name "back". For those with a spouse who has taken their name, there may well be a confusion of expectations about whether they should release the name on divorce, or whether they're entitled to keep it. Essentially, if you want to change it – it's up to you. If you'd like someone else to change it, that's not up to you! Now this may be challenging if your spouse took your name on marriage. While it will have been symbolic on the change, perhaps you would now like them to change it back.

The familial ties and pulls of a name are incredible. Historically we look back at surnames that carry through generations. Surnames are how we find our ancestors when we trace our family history, and how we deduce what they did in their working lives. Biblically, people had appendages on their names to identify them from others – too many Simons meant you needed a second name (Simon Peter) or an identifying characteristic (Simon of Cyrene). Surnames now are a matter of course; everyone has one. Mostly, although not always, surnames are patriarchal – they feed back through the father's line, connecting generations of families.

Did you change or keep your married name?

Carol: I decided to change back to my maiden name and get back to being "me" (I'd allowed myself to be lost a bit during my marriage). As it turned out I began to wish I hadn't as it is such a pain to do… much harder than changing to a married name, I felt. But also, if I'd kept my married name it would have been more useful for a business name – CU Optics would have worked well and CM Optics doesn't have the same ring to it! I should have considered it more rather than just rush in and change it as soon as I could.

Ellie: Initially, I decided to keep my married name because I felt that was who I was at that time. I associated my maiden name more with my teenage years and student days. It was also largely due to being a teacher which meant my name was used throughout the day all the time at work! I didn't want to draw attention to my divorce or feel I needed to explain my circumstances to everyone. However, over a year later when I left my job, I decided it was time to revert to my maiden name. By then it felt like a positive change – "Mrs" had started to make me sound older than I felt and I wanted people to know I was young, free, and single!

May: I use my maiden name for work and still have the married name; when my passport is up for renewal I may change it back.

Rowena: I went back to my maiden name.

I had changed my name on marriage; it was something I was looking forward to doing. So when people knew we were divorcing, some assumed I'd change my name back, some that I wouldn't, and there were a lot of well-meaning "What is your title/surname just so I don't get it wrong because I'd like to send you a card?" questions. And, presumably, it didn't even cross a lot of people's minds!

When it came to my name, I had very firm opinions (this is not a surprise) on what I was doing with it – on both taking my married name and reverting to my maiden one! I had chosen to change my name on marriage because I was looking forward to us becoming a family. For me, that meant sharing a name and I wanted to take his name. So I did.

Changing your title

When we knew we were divorcing, even though many people had asked me, I assumed I would just keep my married name. I'd coasted along nicely with my "Mrs" title and his surname. As a teacher, like Ellie, the change of my surname would have been more intriguing to my class than a lack of wedding ring and therefore not worth the hassle (until I made a career change). I also felt it was *my* name, not his name. My identity had been forged with this name, and I'd been known by it for years. I was determined to retain it; after all, I had made it my own.

The first trigger to change my name was through a discussion with Ellie on this topic. She had decided to change her name back and one of her comments was, "I don't want his name on my [future] marriage certificate." She may not have thought about it since, but it stuck with me. Did I want his surname on a future marriage certificate? Maybe it was my name, but were there also connotations to it that I didn't like?

A second trigger to think through this as-you-were-before scenario was when I bought a train pass and was asked for my title. I ended up with Mrs in the split-second I had to think it through. I had no idea what to say, and I had no idea what I actually wanted to say. I didn't feel like a "Mrs" any more, because I was no longer married, or soon wouldn't be. While I loved changing my name when I got married, and being Mrs, my hesitation before answering any question requiring title and name suggested to me all wasn't quite right with my name retention. Simply put, I didn't want to be Mrs when I wasn't.

As a knee-jerk reaction, I changed my credentials at work to "Ms", because I didn't feel like Mrs. But that didn't fit me either. So, as you will probably have concluded by now, this left me with Miss. Or Lady... Or I could do a PhD and gain "Dr" to avoid the problem entirely, but a) that takes a long time and b) is a lot of work. Alas, I did not, and still do not, have the rights to a title such as Lady. Miss it had to be.

Changing your surname

If I'd had children, I may have felt differently about my surname, wanting to be associated and attached to them through that common bond. But I didn't have any. There was no longer a husband who tied me to that name and with whom I might continue it. That said, I am fortunate not to have an acrimonious relationship with my ex-husband. That isn't easy. Divorce gives abundant potential for point-scoring and recriminations. But cordiality sustained, there was nothing that inspired me to rid myself of my married name as soon as I possibly could.

As I investigated what it would fully mean to change my name, I stumbled across a frequently asked question on a website about name change at the point of divorce. It questioned whether your ex-spouse could force you to change your name – a question I hadn't even entertained. The answer was clear, a little tongue-in-cheek, and feisty (and I therefore liked it). It said names are made up from the letters of the alphabet, and no one owns the alphabet, so no one owns a surname, and therefore no one can make you change it.

This simple sentence completely altered my perspective of "his" name, "my" name, and "our" name. All the letters of the alphabet – a whole myriad of names – and therefore none that were off limits or out of bounds. The concept of pronouns when tied to names was entirely based on my mental picture of it. I began to see possibilities for surnames instead of mine or his.

At this stage I opened the playing field to a few close friends and my brothers, which ended up with a strange variety of unhelpful options, including Ruthie Rainbow (alliterative and a little bit alternative for me) and Ruth Kaleidoscope (autocorrect would have been in constant use).

This is an interesting strategy to try – I wish you more luck than I had. As you may notice from the cover of this book, I didn't take them up on any of these. I am, however, still now, referred to as Ruthie Rainbow Kaleidoscope, so be careful which friends you ask…

Having considered the potential hassle of name change, and "it's a bit of a pain to change it" not being a reason to keep it, it came down to a few key thoughts:

- *Where do I belong?*
- *How do I want to be known?*
- *Who am I now?*

When I got married, together we became a new family unit and changing my surname to his felt completely right to me. One of the great tragedies of divorce is the tearing apart of two families. I belonged also to my mum and dad and my brothers. They – among others – were the ones who were there for me and supported me. When I mentioned reverting to my maiden name, my brothers' response was loving and simple – "You choose. We'll support your decision." Their joint surname was also a pull back towards that feeling of family unity; had there been fewer people with that commonality, I may have felt differently.

Their other slightly less moving comment was, "I never think of you with a surname; you're just Ruth" – which is actually what I wanted to be known as. I just wanted to be known as me, not someone with a backstory to explain on meeting. Just me.

My main reason for not wanting to change back was that I was not the same person I was five years ago when I last held my maiden name. I decided that in taking my name back, I wasn't choosing to go back to being that person. Instead I was choosing to establish myself as a different person: I was choosing to be identified as single and to be content in that – a big deal for me. I was choosing to forge my new identity with an old name. Those who remembered the old name had been with me through thick and thin and often still referred to me by it anyway. Those who've never known it won't associate it with my teenage self but with my new identity. So I decided to embrace my new–old identity.

Questions to consider

How did your name or your spouse's name change on marriage? Why did you choose to do this?

How do you feel about your surname? Consider the reasons you chose to change it on getting married.

Where do you feel you belong?

How do you want to be known?

Who do you feel you are at this stage?

If you're unsure of your name options, ask a couple of close friends to try them out. Whenever they call or text you, ask them to use a particular name. What are your responses to it?

The flipside of being the person choosing whether to change or keep your marital name, is when the choice is not yours. Your spouse may have taken your name, or you may have connected your names on marriage. And you may well have assumptions about what they will do with their name. It may be difficult to countenance that it is not your decision, as indeed the split may not have been. Their changing of their name may feel like a further rejection of you and your marriage. This is a difficult situation, but perhaps consider the above questions from their point of view. Perhaps they too are a different person now, and a new name signifies this to them too.

Relief

I have been tentatively asked whether I was glad, in some ways, that "it" (the divorce) had happened. I knew what was meant by this question – my life was entirely different three and a half years on. I had moved not only job but career, not only house but city; in short, everything was different – and I was loving it. It is highly likely these things would never have happened if I had still been married.

I hope I answered with grace, but I have never been *glad* this happened. For every difficulty and trouble in our marriage, there were joys. I had loved him; I wouldn't have married him if I hadn't. In the same way, I do not have regrets. I am also not relieved or glad to be divorced. It is simply the way things are. Am I glad my life is as it is now? Definitely – but that's asking a different question.

I was relieved, however, once the final paperwork was stamped. It wasn't because I was glad to be divorced, but because the process takes a long time, and regardless of how amicable you are, it is a stressful one. I was relieved that it had concluded, as I would no longer be in a state of "limbo". Divorce and separation is a time of heightened anxiety and tension, so to be relieved at its conclusion is entirely appropriate.

However, it may be that you are relieved to be separated or divorced. There are many circumstances that lead to divorce. Perhaps there was emotional, physical, mental, or sexual abuse within your relationship. Perhaps there were ultimatums to choose between God and your spouse, or threats to your person or your children. To escape from that environment is right, because these things are wrong, and so relief is a natural consequence of escape.

Life changes

So life has changed a lot… and further life changes may be the one thing you are screaming "not that too!" about. Yet the life change of divorce often seems to trigger other change. The two are not intrinsically linked, don't worry! However, divorce provides an opportunity and impetus for reflection that is rather greater than our New Year's resolutions. The overwhelming change to lifestyle, expectations, and dreams as a result of separation and divorce brings a simultaneous freedom of ownership over the next steps and the path your life might take. This can be a frightening, exhilarating, terrifying time. There are bills to pay and responsibility is now being shouldered alone; these are big things to consider, yet there can be a lack of attachment that frees you, like being untethered.

Some changes may be forced upon you. Going back to work or changing jobs to achieve a higher salary might become a necessity now that you are on your own. Moving might be necessary, in order to pay your ex their portion of the home, reduce your rent, or relocate to be nearer family.

Other changes may be a result of one shift bringing about the realization or actualization of a change that has been long thought of, or perhaps the realization that life will not "always be this way".

When considering where to live, there are again many considerations. Often location is linked to community. Sometimes community can be far-flung, with friends living all over the place; sometimes our very closest friends are those we do not see every day. However, having a local community can be extremely valuable when you are emotionally vulnerable or struggling to stay afloat. Staying where you are for your support network may then be a big driver in the decision not to move. When I relocated my place of work to over an hour away in London, I remained living where I was, as I didn't want to uproot both work and home in one go. Once that support network became less immediately needed (though no less loved), I knew I was able to move and eventually did so; my life having become much more centred in the city than where I was previously based.

This support network may also play a part in choosing to move closer to it. If friends and family are mainly located around one area, it may make sense to move in order to have more help with childcare and support for you personally.

The location of your ex-spouse may also play a part in your choice of where to live. If you have children, you may need to allow ease of access to be part of your consideration. This may seem hard – after all, one perk of separation and divorce should be the ability to take only one's own views into account rather than those of both people. Considering it from your children's perspective may help though: can they feel they have easy access to both parental homes?

If you do not have children, or your spouse will not have access, then your ex's location may play a role in a different way. While you live nearby, there is the potential of bumping into them as you run errands or go about your day-to-day life. If you choose to live further away, that chance is naturally decreased. That said, I lived around a five-minute drive from my ex for three years post-separation yet only ran into him once! Not wondering whether you might happen across them has a freeing effect on the mind, and this may again be a positive consideration when deciding whether or not to relocate.

Questions to consider

Where is your support network based?

If you choose to move, would the lack of community have a significant impact on your emotional, physical, or mental health?

How accessible is your ex-spouse's home for your children?

Work is an area of life that may have held many more independent or individual choices. Sometimes location may have limited us, or a need for a particular salary to maintain the family lifestyle, and this may be true now. We may be forced into a return to work for financial reasons, yet separation and divorce offer us the chance to fulfil dreams and pursue career paths that we may have dismissed because of the path our life with our ex was taking. Returning to work may give us the adult conversation we crave or a different support network and group of friends.

Change is, of course, inevitable. And when you have been in a place of unwanted, unexpected change, that can be an uncomfortable place to be. Our attitude to change is one we might have to choose consciously, deliberately developing an attitude that looks forward to possibilities and opportunities, rather than one that looks back at the past or that fears the change of the future. By making choices over the changes wherever we can, we also stop ourselves from fearing change as we make bold decisions concerning our character and mindset. When changes happen to us, our attitudes and responses speak volumes about who we are and who we will be.

Questions to consider

What possible changes in your life excite you?

What possibilities do you see emerging from the separation and divorce?

What are the biggest changes you recognize in yourself or your life since divorce?

Carol: I moved back to a town where I felt part of the community. I started being much more sociable and having fun; I eventually stopped being so angry with God, as I wouldn't have had the businesses or anything had I not married my ex. I also learned an awful lot about alcoholism and other topics, which I believe I will use to help others eventually.

Decobe: As previously mentioned, the biggest change in me is that now I am ME! I'm not the person that marriage had created in me, having to conform to the person that the husband of my wife was meant to be. Rather than partly pretend to enjoy the life that mine had become, I could now be real again. Don't get me wrong, married life wasn't all a sham, parts of it were real and life-enhancing because of being married. But now I'm who I am because I wish to be like that and not because marriage or the world expected it of me. Nowadays my outlook is much more positive and loving.

Ellie: I feel like a different person now. While I am similar in terms of appearance, personality, likes and dislikes, etc., I have learned so much which has impacted how I see myself and how I live. As cheesy as it sounds, I have learned to embrace my feelings, to pursue what I am passionate about, and to be more honest and real with people. Regardless of my relationship status, I feel like I'm more the me I was made to be. Through a horrid experience I learned to accept my weaknesses, lose pride, value vulnerability, and gain empathy. It has definitely helped me to connect more with other people. Although I lost a very important relationship, I am very grateful for the depth of other relationships that have grown through it.

May: I am more at peace now, and settled, as I have my own place to live in. Now rather than hating my ex I want to try to be friends and see him occasionally. I can't forgive everything, just small things that happened, but I just don't think about the bad things, putting the behaviour down to the changed personality resulting from brain damage my ex has. Now I'm hoping to start some new things and get involved in a new neighbourhood where I live. The church I attend has asked me to do a rather large mural, which I may do. However, if I undertake it, I may need something like a sabbatical to complete it!

Rowena: I have now been married again for almost twenty-five years. In that time, I have found faith, and my husband is also a Christian. My marriage is completely different from my first one. Initially, I was probably less trusting and I am quite independent. I probably rely on myself too much.

A few last words...

For all those of us who have experienced divorce and separation, it's not where we expected to be. It was never where we planned or hoped to be. But remember: it's also not the end to your hopes and plans. Gradually or suddenly, intentionally or unintentionally, our lives change, adapt, and alter. More things happen that we never expected; this is stressful and difficult but also incredible and exciting. We meet new people, go to new places, build new memories, and create a new life for ourselves.

Others surprise us, as we surprise ourselves, and the friendships we form as we navigate through this time will become some of the most treasured to remember, as well as some of the most long lasting. We learn how strong we are; our resilience, and our capacity for hope – all of which are far greater than we ever anticipated they'd be.